EXOTIC LIFE

EXOTIC LIFE

LAUGHING RIVERS,
DANCING DRUMS AND
TANGLED HEARTS

LISA ALPINE

A collection of too-true stories

DANCING WORDS PRESS

Dedicated to the ones I love...

My adopted mom, Phyllis Richards McCreery, who swaddled my damaged body and nourished my soul with unconditional love. She is the living embodiment of how being good on the inside reflects outward.

And

My son, Galen Marc Alpine, the biggest and best of all blessings in my life. He is living *la vida fantastica* in the mountains, oceans, and jungles of the world with integrity and passion.

CONTENTS

INTRODUCTION

SHORT STORIES APPEAL to me. I must have a limited attention span. ADHD perhaps? Definitely dyslexic. Maxine Baker, my birth mother, was drunk most of the time she gestated me. Steeped in misery. Anyway, I like to write short, punchy, poignant stories.

I want to spit these stories out the way I tell them to myself. Each one a chocolate bourbon bonbon savored before I go to bed. Sassy and sweet. Sometimes bittersweet, like 82% dark chocolate.

Maybe when I'm older (like cresting ninety?) and more patient, I'll be able to write lengthy intriguing essays about the adventures that have happened, but for now, *gotta* keep going. Another boulder-strewn river to maneuver, another late night tango under an eclipsed moon, another orchard in full blossom to meander.

All these activities I find much more appealing than months spent in the dark cave of my office pecking away, weaving like a spider the legend of my life.

I'm a traveler, a dancer, a writer, a white water kayaker, a gardener, and a book birthing coach. An entrepreneur, a mother, a daughter, a lover, a recluse. These stories are created from the eclectic ingredients of the many aspects and avenues of my life.

I once explained my lifestyle to my writers group, the Wild Writing Women. "It is about getting spilled into the river of life with the knees scraped, the money lost, and the heart broken, yet still getting back into the kayak and paddling forward."

This is my anthology—a word derived from the Greek word for "garland" or "bouquet of flowers."

Here, for you, is a wildflower bouquet from the many seasons of my life.

EXOTIC LIFE

DANCING DIAMONDS

HER SEA GREEN eyes are pointedly focused on me as I sit next to her on the couch. Her dry, cold hand lies over mine, and tightens. I squirm as her platinum wedding band digs into my knucklebones. It hurts.

But she is grinning stiffly at me.

In a measured tone she says, "My dear, I have a gift for you that no one else in the family wants. They are too cheap to insure it so I'm giving it to you, my youngest granddaughter."

My grandmother doesn't give anything without strings attached. Even at ten years old I know this.

My mother and father sit in wingback chairs across the room by the fireplace. They look mystified by this interaction. My grandmother is not a generous person.

"A girl must have this," she says pointedly, as she dramatically reaches behind her back and pulls out an antique black velvet case. My blue eyes become rounder as she inches toward me. Not quite giving it to me, she breathes on me saying, "It was my wedding present from my late husband, Mr. Forbes McCreery. I was very young when I married him. Now it is yours."

The touch of velvet on my palms is like reindeer antlers on a moonlit night in the Arctic. My imagination is awhirl with images of what could be inside.

The top flips open and there lies a delicate lacy diamond shiny glittery necklace.

"It's Victorian," is all she says.

My parents sit in stunned silence. They have never seen this necklace before.

Speechless, I rise from the couch; the velvet case lays flat on my palms like an offering. I skip toward my bedroom and close the door. I gently open the case again and am mesmerized by the twinkle and wink of Austrian cut diamonds and platinum lacework that sparkle against the black velvet.

I place it around my neck and the cold of the diamonds on my skin is exquisite. Shivers of pleasure run through me as I realize it is mine. A fairytale princess necklace that has come true. Rarely in my vast imaginary world do objects actually materialize.

Words are not enough to show my awe at such a gift. Words are dull stones, nothing compared to the intricate beauty of the necklace.

I know what to do to show my grandma how I feel about this gift.

I wrap several silk scarves my mother lets me play with around my slight frame.

"Mama!" I call from my bedroom. "Please put 'Dolly Dawn' on the record player."

Shuffling and muttering sounds come from the living room and then the sunshine pulse of Caribbean steel drums and honey butter voice of Harry

Belafonte heralds my arrival as I snake my way down the dim hallway, entering the living room with a leap and spin. I twirl around the furniture. I shimmy and shake as inspiration grabs me, and one by one I throw the scarves off as I gyrate like a dervish moth in the flame of joy. All that is left on my naked body is the sparkly gorgeous diamond necklace.

Raising my arms up to the heavens in salutation, I turn and bow to my grandma, absolutely convinced I have given her the perfect dance of gratitude.

She sits stiffly upright on the couch, hands tucked lightly under her soft thighs, mouth wide open, gaping like a fish on land. Staring at my exuberant nudity.

She is Victorian, after all.

THE
COPTIC
PRIEST

WHILE SLAVING AWAY at a waitress job in Switzerland in 1973, I read *Exodus* by Leon Uris. The book ignited in me an overwhelming desire to go to Israel, so I saved my money and flew to Tel Aviv. Did I pay attention to the fact that the country had just been at war? No. Did I consider the impact of the recent terrorist massacre of the Israeli Olympic team in Munich? No. Did I worry when I arrived in Tel Aviv in the middle of the night and slept on the linoleum floor at the airport that the bullet holes strafing the wall above my head had been made within the last two weeks? No. I was nineteen years old, blissfully ignorant, and heading for the Promised Land.

As the warm, caramel-colored Middle Eastern sun rose and bathed Israel in morning light, I hitch-hiked to Jerusalem. I stayed at the Methodist hostel in the Old City and spent weeks wandering the alleyways, befriending Palestinian children, old Jewish guards, and Hassidic women at the *hammam* (public steam bath).

I wanted to explore the rest of the country and chose Jericho on the West Bank in the Jordan Valley as my first stop; it is considered by many to be both the oldest city in the world (dating from 7,000 BC) and the lowest city on earth (250 meters below sea level). I hitched a ride south with an Israeli in a noisy tin can of a car. He was horrified that I wanted to go to Jericho and adamantly refused to drive me from the highway into town. He said the Palestinians would rape and rob me and I would never make it out of there alive.

I had him drop me off at the junction and walked into the town of Jericho anyway. I bought plump dates and succulent oranges and sat on a bench, watching dilapidated produce trucks clunk by and short dark women in black dresses zigzag across the plaza, stopping to talk to one another. Jericho was bathed in amber light and warm sun. It felt good on that bench.

I found a guesthouse and rented a room. Then I went for a walk—still no raping or robbing. I walked to the end of a dusty road that led to a tall, mud-brick wall worn down by eons of wind and history. The air caressed my skin; a luscious scent wafted on the whispering silken breeze. The wall surrounded an orange grove and the trees were in full waxy white bloom. The hum of hundreds of bees called me. I scaled the wall, dropped down onto the blossom-covered ground and wandered amid the aisles of trees. The drone of the bees pulled me into a hypnotic state. I lay down, closed my eyes.

When I awoke, a dark-skinned man was sitting directly in front of me. He wore a *keffiyeh*, the traditional Palestinian checked scarf, white and black like Arafat's, and his eyes were bloodshot. He was squatting, arms crossed over his knees. He just stared. I was startled but felt calm. He was calm. He spoke in soft, guttural Arabic, lit up a big newspaper-wrapped spliff and offered it to me. I didn't smoke pot and shook my head. He puffed away and conversed. I had no idea what he was saying but understood he was the orchard guardian. He left me there and I daydreamed as the hills wavered in the heat. It was a timeless, peaceful place.

This became my daily pattern. I wandered the dirt roads leading out of town to the encircling orchard walls of times gone by. I could smell the ancientness, sense the spirits of long-dead residents' robes brushing by me, feel the splendor of great cities bordering the Jordan River. I was a captive of my imagination and I couldn't get enough of that orange-blossom smell.

One day, as I peeked through a gate keyhole in wonder at a particularly fragrant orchard, a man peeked back. The gate opened and there stood the tallest man in Jericho with the biggest ears! He smiled at me and spoke French. Finally, someone I could talk to.

With a grand sweep of his arm, he invited me into his garden. The black robe he wore was frayed and dusty around the edges as it dragged on the ground after him. His orange grove had a unique feature—in the center was an ornate whitewashed church. I had been befriended by a Coptic priest and this was his residence.

We sat in the shade, drinking mint tea, discussing worldly affairs. He had been born in Egypt, where Coptic Christianity originated, and in the course of many exploits he traveled through the Sinai to Israel. His ears waggled as he talked. Suddenly, rocks hit the ground around us, disturbing the harmony of our garden idyll. They were thrown by little boys on the other side of the wall who were walking home from school. The boys tormented the priest because he wouldn't let them play in the grove. He scurried out the gate and chased them down the road, cursing them, his robes stirring up great billowing clouds of bone-dry dust.

This turned out to be a daily occurrence during our visits when I found myself in his garden, listening to stories of his very long life.

On Sunday I dressed up and went to church. I knocked on the wooden gate. The Coptic priest was splendidly attired in a clean robe. Massive ornate silver crosses hung around his neck, and his head was topped with a tall, pointed stiff hat. He ceremoniously led me inside the church. It was dark and small, musty and mysterious; paintings of gilded saints loomed on the walls over the altar.

There was one other person inside, a wizened old lady in black, kneeling and praying. Audibly. My friend commenced the service by lighting a gigantic copper incense burner that he swung around and around. As it built up momentum, he circumambulated the miniature room. Billows of intensely pungent copal fumes filled the church. They became so thick, I couldn't see my hand. The clouds of sickly sweet smoke wrapped around like a boa constrictor and choked me. Through the haze I heard him chanting in a dominant voice. He refused to put down the incense burner. I was dying from smoke inhalation but felt obligated to stick it out and support him as part of his congregation of two—perhaps the only Christians in a sea of Muslims who would tolerate his penchant for ancient, murky rituals.

Two weeks passed, and another church service. I was becoming a fixture in Jericho. The women in town befriended me on my daily meanderings through the market and plaza. I became an object of lunch invitations and unintentionally initiated a town-wide competition to see who could make the most delectable *Ma'aluba*, a greasy lamb and rice dish that was not delectable at all since I was a vegetarian. However, I could not refuse their hospitality, so I had lunch many times a day. These abundantly wide women wanted to fatten me up and marry me off to one of their sons who, luckily for me, were all off studying at the university.

As if part of the conspiracy to increase my girth, the Coptic priest was always plying me with drippy, syrupy sweets and tree-plucked oranges. In spite of this fact, we became good friends. I trusted him and he never took advantage of me. In fact, no one did.

I felt protected and watched over in Jericho. What more could one ask as a guest in someone's country? I was not a woman to exploit, a pocket to rob, or an American to hate. I was just the blond traveler from California sitting on a park bench eating dates, savoring the sweet, moist, nutritious fruits that have been nurtured for millennia in the oldest town on this earth.

AMAZON MOM

MY FIRST EXPERIENCE as a mom was in the Amazon in 1975 when I was twenty-one. I got a village of Indians plastered and they abandoned their kids to my care.

I had unintentionally purchased this maternal role for the price of one dollar. All I thought I was buying for that corruptible buck was the use of a dugout canoe. I wanted to explore the banks of the Rio Napo, possibly to find a dolphin-inhabited lagoon or silently glide close to a turtle in its muddy burrow, or even pass under a boa lethargically wound around an overhanging branch. Stuff like that.

The novel *Green Mansions* had awakened in me an incredible desire to travel the waterways of the Amazon basin and penetrate its green veil. After I'd saved two thousand dollars while working six months for a record company in San Francisco, I quit my job and flew to South America.

On a map, it looked like the Rio Napo would lead me to the Amazon. I began my journey on a rattletrap bus over the Ecuadorian Andes and into the Oriente rainforest where the Napo snakes its way to join the Amazon River near Iquitos, in Peru.

Luckily, I was in no hurry and could hitch boat rides. There is an unspoken rule of hospitality among the people in the rainforest who live in open-sided huts on stilts along the riverbank. Travelers are welcome to sleep in their houses because the jungle floor is far too dangerous at night. Even the floor of the hut where I slept the first night was horrifyingly alive. When darkness fell, creatures began to torment me. Vampire bats, which I'd always thought were a myth, dive-bombed my head, looking for places to attach themselves for their nightly fill of blood. After injecting an anesthetic into their unaware host, they are free to suck away. They prefer toes and noses; other travelers I met had alarming stories of waking up with puncture marks on the tips of their noses.

Then, a creature I will never be able to identify ran back and forth over me. It seemed to have claws like a chicken and it made snuffly rodent sounds. I curled up under my rain poncho and sweated out that first night. At dawn, I approached my Indian hosts and begged them to sell me one of their hammocks. Anything to get off the ground!

With my new hammock and a sheet of plastic in which I could wrap myself up each night like a burrito—safe from critters, but steamy hot—I continued down the Rio Napo, first with the postmaster on his monthly mail run, then with a trader. Each progressive *panga* (dugout canoe) got smaller and the motors fewer as I traveled deeper into the jungle. My forward pace came to a standstill in Pantoja, on the Peruvian border. Due to territorial conflicts between Ecuador and Peru, there were no more boats traveling downriver.

I was stuck in Pantoja for two weeks. The villagers were reserved and suspicious, but allowed me to hang my hammock in an abandoned hut. The last occupant had recently died. He had fallen out of his boat in the middle of the river and a neighbor explained, "One of those big-mouth fish ate him." I made a mental note not to swim in the river.

I offered the man in the hut next to mine money in exchange for the use of his canoe. I had already asked if his family would keep a pot of water boiling continuously on the fire for me after I discovered that the river was not only the source of their drinking water, but also their toilet. No Perrier around here! I felt I should give him something for any other extra favors. When I waved an Ecuadorian bank note in front of him, he looked puzzled. Canoe rentals were a new concept and it looked like money was too. They had no use for cash—there were no stores, and the passing traders took animal hides and dried fish for payment. In the end, however, he finally took my money.

I now had an activity to pass the time. I'd already attempted to tag along with the village hunter a few days before, but keeping up with him in the web-like jungle was exhausting. He ran low to the ground with his five-foot blowgun at his side. The vine-tangled canopy made the forest oppressively hot, buggy and slippery. I knew I couldn't keep up with him, so I abandoned any romantic vision of watching him hunt down a jaguar or thirty-foot snake, and headed back to the village alone.

Paddling the tipsy, cracked canoe turned out to be another frustrating experience. The river's current was unexpectedly strong, the sun merciless. Perhaps the hammock, with its nylon cords that cut into my back, wasn't such a bad place to spend the afternoons. I abandoned the canoe and headed back to my hut where I parked myself with a book, twice read and dog-eared, in the hammock.

Then the children appeared. Suddenly, I was popular. They were approaching instead of hiding from me as they normally did. By ones and twos, they'd climb or crawl up the splintery steps and peer at me with big, dark eyes. No smiles, just stares. The small ones gripped the hands of their older siblings. I swung back and forth, the hammock rope creaking, cutting a groove into the beams. The kids inched forward.

Soon this baker's dozen of kids, aged two to fourteen, were yanking the hammock to get it to swing higher. The little ones crawled into its banana peel shape with me. Giggles, tickles, chasing. They took over my hut and didn't leave. It felt like a day care center run by the *Cat in the Hat*.

One melancholy-eyed girl picked up my hairbrush and stroked my blond hair. The other girls gathered around. Lubina, of the sad eyes, pulled my blouse forward and peered down the front. She shook her head in disbelief and announced that I was "white all over!" in pidgin Spanish. They each took a peek and had the same incredulous reaction. At dusk, the kids still filled my house. Dinner. What about dinner? I didn't want to eat my can of tuna fish, which I usually just scooped into my mouth on the end of a Swiss Army knife. There wasn't enough to go around, so it was oatmeal for everybody. They scurried over the banister and down the steps to get their bowls. Iridescent blue clouds of thirsty Morpho butterflies exploded upward from the puddle edges as the children stormed past.

I went to my neighbor's hut to get some water. The windowless interior was pitch black. Snorting punctuated the darkness. Raucous laughter rose toward me from the floor as I tripped over something. I lit a match and illuminated a huddle of thigh-slapping villagers, all howling as they pointed at me. Apparently I was the funniest thing they had ever seen.

They were rip-roaring drunk, thanks to me. Mr. Canoe Rental had turned his tidy fee into enough cane alcohol to get every adult in the village drunk for several days. He'd paddled like a demon to the Peruvian military outpost (consisting of one shack, two soldiers) and brought back a huge jug of the extremely potent local brew.

I didn't mind being laughed at—that was nothing new—but I felt guilty. I had corrupted this capital-free village with my measly buck. I was the snake in Rousseau's garden.

It became apparent why the kids had clustered around me. They needed me. Someone had to care for them while their parents lolled about, bathed in tears of mirth. No mean drunks here, just comedians.

The adults were on their drunken sabbatical for several days. I got used to living with a dozen kids.

I felt responsible for them and they were very affectionate with me. I developed mothering skills I didn't know I had. I told them children's stories in a language they didn't speak. I cuddled the little ones and made a bed for them in my hammock. I cooked odd stews of dried *Pirarucú* (delicious fresh water fish) and smoked monkey meat. Together we washed our clothes in the river from log rafts. They showed me where it was safe to swim. We splashed and dived and painted our bodies with green-grey clay from the riverbanks. My dreams of heading toward Brazil had drifted away. I forgot my downstream quest.

By this time the adults had exhausted their alcohol. They were sober and back on track, but the kids still stayed overnight and hung out with me during the day. Lubina walked about in my over-sized clothes and looked like Minnie Mouse strutting around with a pair of my high heels on her tiny feet. I had become fond of her and I had fantasies of bringing her home with me.

Then, a military seaplane landed in front of our village. Suddenly, there was transportation available and I had to decide quickly if I wanted to accept an offer of a ride. The pilot was shocked to find an American woman in such a remote outpost and felt obligated to airlift me to Iquitos.

I hurriedly packed and in the hubbub of an abrupt departure, I didn't feel the tearing sense of leaving the children behind until the plane was circling over the village and I knew I would never be there again.

The jungle is amazing from overhead. River tributaries twist like Shiva's arms through the green tangle. So much water, so much growth. So far away. I hear that the Rio Napo has been destroyed by oil spills over the last decade. Lubina and the children of Pantoja are adults now. I wonder where they live if they can live there no longer.

SOLE
FOOD

I WAS TRAVELING OVER the Altiplano on a gravel road that snakes around Lake Titicaca in Bolivia. The Indians there are extremely poor and the environment absurdly harsh (13,000 feet elevation and freezing). There are no tourist facilities so I spent the night in an Aymara Indian family's mud brick hut. I was hungry. They invited me to dine with them.

They were eating what they ate every day of the year—*chuños*, tiny freeze-dried potatoes in weird mottled colors of purple, green, and red. The potato originated in South America and there are more varieties in Bolivia and Peru than any other part of the world. The dehydrated ones we were eating had been reconstituted with murky boiling water. No salt. No flavor. My hosts savored them. These puny potatoes were a main part of their existence. When they weren't eating them, they were cultivating them.

"How are they harvested?" I asked to spark conversation among this very reticent and superstitious family. The mother, whose mahogany face was cracked and polished from exposure to extreme weather, told me, "We dig them up when they are ready and leave them on the hard ground to freeze. Then we go through the field in our bare feet and roll each one under our feet to remove the skin. We store them in baskets and they last a year."

"Oh," was my only comment.

I looked down at her feet. They were blackened and cracked and had calluses as thick as history books.

Maybe I did detect some flavor in my meal after all...

THE DWARF
AND
THE OTTER

"WHERE IS YOUR favorite place in all the countries you've visited?" This question is asked of me frequently. Without a second's hesitation I always answer, "Chiloé." Then a deep longing to return there washes over me. Always.

I discovered this remote island in Patagonia by accident. The cattle boat a friend and I were traveling on from Punta Arenas in Argentina to Puerto Montt in Chile stopped there briefly.

It had been a tumultuous weeklong trip in the hold of a rusty cargo ship. The boat only ran this route during the calmer "summer" season and this was its last outing until the following spring. Winter squalls were edging in and the seas were getting rough. During that voyage I never saw a smooth horizon or a straight angle. The boat was tossed around like a bipolar cork. Throwing up was *de riguer* even for the hardened crew. The predecessor of this fine vessel was pointed out to me one sleet-pounding day. A wizened man in a knit cap lifted his gnarled finger toward a dark shape rising from a misty curtain of wave froth off the stern. There she was, the sister ship, bow toward the heavens, sunken by heavy wave action just the previous season—a monument to our collective queasiness.

Due to my subsistence-level travel budget, I was in economy class along with several dozen Patagonian peasants in the bow of the boat. Sleeping with fifty others in a dank, enclosed boat hold is…intimate. Hand-loomed woolen clothes that rarely got washed perfumed our living quarters with a tangy mutton aroma. The seven-dollar fare included not only bunk bed accommodations and transport, but also meals, all of which consisted of mussel soup with nutritional seaweed clinging like old beards to the shells. No amount of soaking in the hairy broth softened the accompanying hardtack.

Most of my fellow passengers were missing half their teeth—probably from gnawing on those petrified biscuits. Not only did I not gain an ounce of weight but I had the good fortune to inherit tapeworms from my toothless companions. If you ever want to drop a lot of weight fast *and* eat anything and everything in sight at the same time, consign a tapeworm.

My traveling compatriot from California and I decided we needed some sort of friendship offering to breach the differences with our shipmates. What better way to melt cultural and communication barriers than with alcohol? Before we boarded, we invested in several fifty-litre jugs of Argentinean plonk—cheap red table wine. I was enamored with the quaint hand-blown green glass jugs encased in sturdy wicker baskets with hefty branch handles. We stowed the vino beside our bunk and drank it every night with the perennial briny mussel soup.

Did I mention where they got the mussels? One morning when I was, yet again, leaning over the gunwale retching while trying not to get tossed into the sea, I witnessed the galley knaves scraping mollusks off the exterior hull. Hmmm. I didn't know they did boat cleaning at sea. I thought they did it in drydocks. I soon learned that the prep cooks were braving their lives to harvest our next meal. How convenient to be using our watercraft for transport *and* a sustainable food source.

Washing this questionable menu item down with vast quantities of red wine was commendable—and necessary. We shared our stash with our fifty peasant buddies. This made us extremely popular—the downside being that our two tin cups turned out to be the *only* cups in economy class. So we passed them around—hence the tapeworms. Share and share alike.

The other thing we had to share was music. We had brought along an old creaky tape recorder and cassette tapes (remember them?). As the dented cups passed from weathered lips to more leathered lips, we cranked up The Rolling Stones. The peasants went wild. They hadn't grown up doing the Twist, the Monkey, the Funky Chicken, or the Frug; they danced the *Cueca*—a Chilean courtship dance wherein the men spun a handkerchief over their heads and stamped their feet as the women swirled coquettishly around them. Our shipmates adapted this folk dance to "Jumping Jack Flash." We'd carry on every night. It was like a disco—dark, crowded, noisy, drunken. The festive spirit was contagious. Even the cattle in the hold next to us kicked the bulkhead in time to the music like hoofed bongo drummers.

The crew invited my friend and me to stick around and become their floorshow the next season. Tempting, but...

This way of traveling north from Tierra del Fuego up the Patagonian fjords was the only way to reach Puerto Montt from the southern latitudes. Today, there are roads and tourists, seaplanes and luxury expedition boats, but in 1974 it was cattle boat or swim.

I first saw Chiloé when the boat stopped to drop off its straggly cattle herd on the dock at Quellón on the southern tip of the island. Darwin spent the summer of 1835 here on the Beagle to study the abundant marine life.

It was one of our rare times off the boat that week. Once I found my landlubber legs, I wandered into the village hoping for a meal of anything but mussels. In a dusty shop window were hand knit sweaters in subtle natural tones of berry and moss, mushroom and lichen. For three dollars I bought one with a cozy cowl collar and hand-carved bone buttons.

That durable sweater traveled all over South America with me for the next six months. It even changed my destiny.

I eventually got back to San Francisco and, while wandering around Fisherman's Wharf looking for a job, I passed a door with a sign that read Buyer's Entrance. Why I pushed that door open and went up the dingy stairwell is still a mystery. The stairs led me to an office and when the Cost Plus receptionist asked me why I was there I replied, "I'd like to see the sweater buyer."

Two minutes later, I was standing in front of the desk of a very nice woman who looked at me quizzically. I modeled my sweater; yes, the one that, since

Quellón, had served as a pillow on Bolivian busses and a blanket on snow-covered volcanic peaks in Ecuador. She said matter-of-factly, "I'll take 300, 60 days, net 10, FOB, in small, medium and large."

Alrighty then...

With not a clue as to what she meant, I wrote it down phonetically, hoping to make sense of it later.

Once I deciphered what she had ordered, I realized I had just started an import company.

With the Cost Plus purchase order in my hand, I needed funding since my bank account had maybe $100 in it. I marched right in to the newly opened Women's Bank in the Financial District. The women executives in dark suits and moderate pumps laughed at me. Really! Here I was, a young woman starting a promising career and they turned up their surgically sculpted noses and mocked me. So what if I was wearing Birkenstocks and a flower-print skirt? It was infuriating. Fuming, I continued to stomp down the street. A flashing neon sign caught my eye, "Free cookbooks with every new savings account opened." "Wow," I thought, "Promising. If nothing else, I'll get a cookbook."

This is how I ended up returning to Chiloé a week later with a $10,000 loan from a black businessmen's bank (go figure). The cookbook was an extra perk.

Getting to Chiloé from the north was a tad easier than from the south. It only required a flight to Santiago, Chile; a twelve-hour train ride to Puerto Montt; a long ferry ride across the choppy waters of the Chacao Strait; and a five-hour bus ride. Thank God I was twenty-two years old with the digestive tract of a mule and the flexibility of a Chinese acrobat who needed very little sleep.

I hadn't really considered the possibility that there might not even be 300 sweaters in small, medium, and large on the entire island—or enough people to knit them. Fortunately, *everybody* there knitted. It was a regional pastime. Suddenly I was the messiah bringing cash for something the locals hadn't ever considered a commodity.

That first order launched my company, Dream Weaver Imports. Soon, I was trekking back and forth to Chile, Bolivia, Ecuador, Peru, Colombia and the Amazon buying all manner of oddities and apparel for my wholesale and retail businesses. In less than three years I had two retail stores, eight employees and a vast wholesale business. So there, Women's Bank!

Anyway...

On one of my quarterly buying trips to Chiloé, I went to the wharf in the village of Dalcahue to have a quiet meal after schlepping sweaters from outlying farmhouses into town all day by horse cart. A crisp Chilean sauvignon blanc accompanied chilled sea conch salad (more delicious than its cousin, abalone) and a stew redolent with sea bass and *congrio* (eel). I asked the cook to hold the mussels.

I was deciphering a newspaper when a shadow loomed over the newsprint. I looked up and there was a dwarf staring at me like I was some kind of freak. Tourists were still a rarity in these parts.

"Are you American?" he asked in perfect English. It was awkward speaking in my own language after so many days haltingly communicating in Tsesungún, the local dialect, so I just shook my head affirmatively.

This was the beginning of one of the oddest relationships I've ever had.

After a long existential philosophy debate over wine—a lot of wine—I agreed it was a grand idea for me to tag along with the dwarf on a fishing trip to the outer islands of the Chiloean Archipelago. He said he wanted to practice his English and that he was leaving immediately.

This was the moment when reality, folklore, and common sense blurred, sweeping me up on a magical mystery tour of mapless islands and fjords carved out by the Quaternary glaciers.

Without even checking his boat to make sure it could float or a concern about my tight buying trip schedule, I threw my belongings on deck and off we sailed.

The first evening as I was fending off the advances of my drunken captain (who had started being offensive as soon as we left port), a growling meow sound from behind made us pause in our verbal wrangling over why I didn't want to sleep in his bed. A creature with four legs and opaque obsidian eyes, blanketed in shiny dark wet fur, scurried between my legs.

Oh my god, a wild sea otter! The dwarf yelled at it but it sashayed right through the open door of the cabin and burrowed into the tangle of blankets on the dwarf's bed. It turned out the otter was a regular visitor and apparently viewed me as the intruder.

The dwarf and I came to an understanding very quickly. I would listen to his poems and the stories he wove about the mythology of Chiloé, but *no no no* on the hootchy-koo. And no pouting about it, either! He was a very moody little guy.

For the next several nights I lashed myself, wound in a cocoon of scratchy blankets, to the deck. And every evening the musky otter galumphed over me in order to cuddle up with the dwarf. This sleeping arrangement seemed to work for everybody.

Ostensibly, this was a fishing expedition but I never saw our captain throw a net or cast a line. The otter caught more fish than we did.

During the day as we chugged between islands, the dwarf recited poetry to his captive audience: me. His poems were swathed in angst and anger.

His father was a renowned Chilean poet who had disappeared under General Pinochet's directive. The dwarf had also been detained within the last year by the military Junta, stuffed into a burlap sack and kicked to death. Or so the soldiers thought.

Now the dwarf was hiding out on a fishing boat in the waterways of islands, viewed as forgotten. It was not a large boat and he was a very passionate man. Deflection became my modality, yet I was attracted to and repulsed by him at the same time. His feudal behavior and primitive ways fit this strangely-lit terrain like a song.

The landscape of rolling moss green hills licked by the steel black-blue sea had the qualities of a dusty seventeenth-century Dutch master oil painting. During the day, a pallid light illuminated the mostly uninhabited sheep-strewn atolls. I loved the solitude and dreamy opaqueness of this region. It spoke to parts of me that were normally veiled behind the fast-paced international business life I led. Being with this temperamental poet inspired me to journal and photograph, attempting to capture Chiloé's surreal, shadowy lure, and losing myself to the place in the process. It turned me inside out, bringing to the forefront of my awareness the mystical dreamscapes I inhabited as a child. I was even beginning to feel proportionally smaller. His size. Condensed down to his intense perspective.

We'd troll silently through the early morning mist that hovered over the waterways between these specks of islands. The dwarf would suddenly pause and stare with great intent toward the horizon. He would point and ask me to look in the direction he was indicating. Slowly, he'd unwind the myth about a ghost ship and how it warned seafarers to turn back toward land and away from the open seas.

As he told the tale in a barely audible whisper, I'd see fragments of a ship's silhouette in the distance. We both knew it was a message not to travel any farther south. Obediently, we'd turn to the shores of some barren isle and moor, asking the local fishermen for sustenance.

The atmosphere inside their huts perched on the ragged rocky shore was dense with the fumes of smoky peat and stale dried conch. Some nights I'd sleep on the dirt floor of these huts just to escape the dwarf's yearning and loneliness and the stench of the lovelorn sea otter.

Our ten-day sojourn did end, with the dwarf leaving me and my belongings back on the wharf in Dalcahue. He pulled anchor and went into hiding again. I gathered up my stock of sweaters sewn into flour sacks and traveled north.

DRIED FISH AND IMPULSIVE LOVE

I SMELLED LIKE DRIED fish. As I sat in a coffeehouse in Bogotá, the sharp pieces of dried fish that clung to my cotton trousers were scratchy and annoying. The hard plastic chair—a neon shade of Orange Julius orange—pressed the bits deeper into my flesh. I squirmed with discomfort but then I looked at Bob and felt ecstatic.

Warm coffee. Cool mountain air. Such pleasantness on my skin after weeks in the steamy, prickly, bug-scratching jungle.

Usually I traveled alone on my import/export journeys when I collected unusual artifacts for my wholesale business and retail stores in California. Puddle jumping on prop planes from Bogotá into the heart—the artery—of the Amazon Basin to Leticia is not for those who like the comforts of first class travel. No one appreciates mosquitoes.

But I didn't mind them or the staph-infected bites and the scars they left on my arms and legs after every trip south. They were merit badges. Evidence of survival and adventure. Malaria, piranhas, drug lords, lecherous men. I always returned home in one piece—well, almost—after the mosquitoes had taken their *mordida*.

What was I doing bringing a boyfriend with me on this trip? Bob was dreadful, too. He hated the jungle and despised the Indians I traded with. Couldn't even paddle a canoe or take a photograph. He was in a constant state of hypochondriacal hysteria no matter how glorious the gigantic (two meters in diameter) Reina Victoria lily pads were—each one a universe inhabited by jade-green frogs and giant-legged bugs—or how strange and mythical the pink river dolphins appeared, quietly rising up and sinking back into the inky waters as our canoe wove through the tangle of vines and roots. I was so grateful to see this through our Indian guide's eyes. Bob was not.

It seemed incongruous because I was Scandinavian-blond and delicate in appearance and he, Bob Duncan (an odd name for a Chinese guy from San Francisco), looked swarthy and indigenous, even though he was a strikingly handsome mutt mix of Chinese and Scottish.

This nasty, whiny, jet-black haired boyfriend and I escaped back up to Bogotá. Cool, refreshing Bogotá, in a cargo plane loaded with dried Amazonian river fish. We perched atop planks of the stinky, sun-dried fish in an un-pressurized cabin. The planks were our seats. He quacked so loud I could hear his complaints over the propeller's incessant bronchial roar.

The pilot forced us to get out on the runway when we landed. We had to jump out as the plane was still taxiing. He was not supposed to have passengers—just fish. We scrambled across the tarmac, hopped a chain link fence and flagged down a bus

to town. We were so stinky it was no problem getting a seat, as the passengers gave us lots of room.

So here we sat, together, over a cup of Colombian
coffee in a modern plastic cafeteria. Bob, whom I
wanted to push out of the airplane at high altitude
less than an hour ago, suddenly looked delicious.
His taunting eyes flashing at me, rich umber silken
skin under my fingers, a song in his eyes as he felt
my light touch. His slightly torn plaid shirt hung off
his broad shoulders. Black black black straight hair.

Suddenly, I wanted to marry this man. This Bob
Duncan man. This horse trainer from home whom
I'd met six months ago at a dude ranch in Men-
docino and didn't even like when we first met. My
chest was humming with love as I drank him in. I'd
never felt like marrying anyone in all of my twenty-
four years on this planet. Before. Ever. It had never
occurred to me to get married.

He read my mind and proposed over the tiny cup
of *café tinto* . Was it the intoxicating dizzying effect
of the fish smell—an aphrodisiac that only we had
just discovered? Some magic potion the *curanderos*
(healers or witchdoctors) sell in the herb markets

to weave a spell of love? Had we stumbled upon the "smell of love"?

Whatever spell or vapor or Mars-in-retrograde caused us to impulsively commit to spending the rest of our days together in marital bliss only lasted long enough for me to write a rosy letter about our future to my parents.

My poor parents. A daughter roaming the world to places they wouldn't dream of traveling to—and she by herself. Finally, a man to take care of her! Alas, two weeks later when we arrived back in California, they were waiting for us at the terminal gate with a dozen red roses and a bottle of French champagne.

My father, ever the Old World charmer, said, "Come, let's celebrate this joyful news of your marriage."

"What are you talking about?" I was truly mystified.

My parents nodded and smiled knowingly at Bob with a look that said, "Now you get to deal with her whimsical, fickle nature."

The letter. I had forgotten about the proclamation of love I had written about to them in that far away coffeehouse in Bogotá during that lull in our argumentative storm that tricked us into thinking we actually loved each other. The stink of the dried fish suddenly filled my nostrils and I remembered the proposal that wore off within a day of delivery. Quicker than the fish smell and with less of a trace.

This was the last trip I invited Bob on.

It is a good thing I did not marry him. I found out there were more differences between us than taste in travel. He turned out to be abusive—and a drug addict. Not qualities one wants in a husband.

SPIRITUAL GRACE UNDER A BLUE-BLACK SKY

THERE IS A dance tonight. There is one almost every night somewhere in Bali. I wrap a sarong around me, hold it up with a sash and wear a shirt that covers my arms. I do not want to offend the Balinese if the dance I'm going to attend should be held in a temple courtyard tonight.

I step out from my hut under a blue-black velvet sky set with sparkling diamond stars. The Balinese evening makes a sensuous tapestry. Incense, clove cigarettes and cooking spices mix with the heavy perfume of night-blooming flowers. The scents fill the still evening air and have an intoxicating effect on me.

Listening for a faint tinkling of music in the distance, I walk narrow dirt paths through the rice paddies. Deep-throated frogs keep time with my footsteps. Fireflies light my way.

The crash of cymbals becomes distinct, and the shadows of people appear, all wandering in the same direction. As I enter the village, kerosene lamps shine from doorways and catch the glimmer of gold threads woven into the sarongs worn on the lean, brown bodies of people moving toward the festivities.

We all head for the dance performance rumored to occur in this small village tonight, a night lit by a full blue moon. Its round face reflects in silver ripples on a multitude of flooded rice terraces, a moon that, as it rises, creates long black shadows along the path.

Among the surrounding villages, I've heard talk spreading about who would be performing at tonight's ceremonies. Will it be the humorous Topeng mask actor from Mas, the acclaimed dancer of the

Kebyar from Peliatan, the particularly flirtatious and sinuous Oleg dancer from Ubud, or the young master of the Baris from the village where we are going tonight? Young and old come to see the classic dances they know by heart and have seen retold countless times in a hundred slightly different ways. The *bale banjar* (community hall) is ablaze with kerosene lamps and alive with the hum and rustle of the village population milling about. We crowd onto hand-hewn wood benches to get a close-up look. I attract attention with my blond hair and blue eyes, especially from the children, who titter and flash me huge smiles. All of them have an appealing, mischievous twinkle in their eyes. Several matronly types approach and take the friendly liberty of retying my sarong properly. In their eyes I wrap it very awkwardly. Somehow, my big Western body doesn't look as graceful as theirs with this rainbow-hued cloth twisted around it. The fabric doesn't drape the same way on me as on their delicate frames. I am offered sweets and tea—no introductions, just village warmth. They are pleased a Westerner is interested in their village performance and has come showing respect by wearing traditional dress.

The gamelan orchestra warms up, and then, with a resounding crash, forty metal hammers hit the iron keys of the gamelan instruments in unison. This abrupt sound sends a jolt up my spine and seizes my attention. The trembling stage curtains part and out strides a Baris dancer in bejeweled attire, his feet stomping, eyes flashing and hands fluttering in rapid gestures. The movements of the Baris dance represent male strength, courage and resolve, the epitome of the warrior in the eyes of the Balinese.

Posturing brave stances with sweat gleaming on his brow, the young Baris dancer regally turns about and disappears. The music calms and softens; bells and the tinkle of the gamelan set the mood of the next dance. Fluttering fans appear from behind the curtains, followed by two charming butterfly-like creatures. The famous Legong dance has begun. The two tiny dancers sway and undulate, dip and turn, following the motion of their hand-held fans. These dazzling Legong dancers are the female counterpart of the Baris portrayal of the Balinese warrior spirit. They are like exquisite swaying flowers in full regalia of royal green and gold brocade. Crowns of frangipani blossoms frame their perfect features. Their delicate young bodies are bound tightly in swathes of rich silk.

These girls are chosen at five-to-seven-years-old for their attractive features and matching appearances. They are then trained in the manners of Legong. In the days of Balinese princely states, these girls were usually future wives of the rulers. The Legong dancers are viewed as the quintessence of femininity and grace in Balinese society.

The brilliance of the elaborate costumes, expressive masks and ornate headdresses combined with the well-trained, fluid movements of the dancers enrapture me. It is almost too much splendor for my eyes to behold, yet it is presented in such a simple setting.

This evening, like many other festival nights in Bali, features a potpourri of dances covering a wide range of styles, from comedy to masked tragedy to fiery, passionate depictions of love and war. The performers are as much actors as dancers, relying on eloquent facial expressions, often with very little movement of their bodies.

Dance is alive and flourishing in every corner of the island. There are more than fifty different dances and two hundred dance troupes. The villagers are proud of the arts, and this abundant creativity is shared with the community. The generosity of artistic spirit has inspired a fertile breeding ground for new versions of the dances as creative juices are plowed back into the soil of the community.

Most Balinese dances are created to appease and entertain the deities. The dramatic arts offer a means of cleansing the village by strengthening its resistance to harmful forces through offerings, prayers and acts of exorcism. Balinese dance strives to establish a middle ground—a harmony between two opposite poles. The moral message is clear to any Balinese child: good and evil are ever present; the fight for good requires the strength of a warrior and constant awareness of right actions, plus offerings to appease the deities on both sides of the fence.

Many dances include trance states. Trances are a common means for the Balinese to honor their gods by offering their bodies as vessels to the spirits and their messages. Probably the most spectacular of the trance dances is the Sanghyang Jaran.

For the Sanghyang, a large pile of coconut husks is lit in the center of the performing area. The burning mound of shells turns into a crackling fire emanating such intense heat that I break out into a sweat. When the embers are bright red, men spread the hot coals over the ground. The gamelan orchestra strikes a dynamic chord that makes me jump off my seat. The clash and clatter of sound announces the dramatic appearance of a barely-clad man on a wooden horse who gallops across the fiery carpet of glowing coals. We gasp again as he turns his stick steed about and charges once more into the heat. This time, he stops abruptly in the center, kicking burning embers in every direction. The dancer is overcome by his zealous trance state. He grins, then shouts and races this way and that, chasing evil demons that only he can see. His ecstatic fervor will go on until the priest recognizes that it is time to draw the man back to consciousness.

Another example of a dance performed tonight that invokes a devotional warrior state is the Kris (dagger) dance. Rangda, queen of the witches, is the most vicious and evil of the demon gods. Her straggly hair, pendulous breasts, and drooling mouth portray vileness. The she-witch enters the bodies of the Kris dancers, who represent the community. Under her destructive influence the men, in a trance, turn their own daggers against themselves. I find myself anxiously biting my nails as they dig the sword points into their bare chests. Again, the priest helps pull them back so that good may win. Then, the mighty Barong, protector of humanity and similar to a Chinese dragon in appearance, marches down the steps in the last scene to triumph over the nasty, horrifying Rangda and her foul cohorts.

The battle between light and dark is abated for the moment, and balance has been achieved between the opposing forces of good and evil. We exhale a collective sigh of relief. Children pile off the wooden benches, acting out some of the more gruesome scenes. We all gather around the food vendors waiting just beyond the halo of the kerosene lamps.

As I walk home late into the night, my hands flutter and arc casting dancing shadows on the ground, unconsciously imitating the graceful motions of those refined dancers.

MADDENING MEANDERINGS IN MADAGASCAR

THE PROSTITUTES THOUGHT our son Galen was a real gentleman. In fact, maybe the only gentleman (besides his father) in the crowd dining *al fresco* in front of the Hotel du France in Antananarivo.

This was our first night in the capital of Madagascar after a flight from Nairobi. At the suggestion of a fellow traveler, we had added this stop to a safari trip in Kenya. It took a while for us to realize that the well-heeled, Levi-clad young girls milling around us in the restaurant were plying their trade. Packs of hungry-eyed children clustered behind the iron fence separating the patio from the sidewalk. The girls passed food and money to the youngsters—family members waiting to be fed. While the girls waited for men to consign their services, they bounced our blond, blue-eyed three-year-old on their knees. Cutest Westerner they'd ever seen.

That night, when we bedded down in our room, haunting sounds of creaking springs and frequent groans seeped through the walls. Sleep eluded us as deep male grunts confirmed our suspicions that this hotel was not on the *Relais et Chateaux* route.

At 6:00 a.m. the following morning, we shuffled off to the train station and set out to explore the mysteries of Madagascar in a 19th century "iron horse." Late in the day, we disembarked at Perinet, on the edge of a lemur preserve, and checked into a dilapidated hotel next to the train station.

One of the wonders that lured us to Madagascar was its prolific and unique flora and fauna. This red-earth island, 250 miles off the coast of East Africa, is the place to find grotesquely shaped Baobab trees, mysterious underwater coelacanths (fish once thought to be extinct), and mouse lemurs, the smallest primates in the world.

A guide led us into the rainforest looking for indri-indri, one of thirty-three lemur species found only in Madagascar. Treading for miles beneath the dense canopy, we craned our necks looking for this endangered and elusive lemur, which sleeps eighteen hours a day. Finally, several indri-indri stirred the canopy a hundred feet overhead, and we were treated to a brief glimpse of furry behinds.

The next morning, my intrepid husband felt the lure of the lemur and took off again with the guide into the yawning green. Galen and I chose to explore a local village. We found a town near the train tracks and were soon surrounded by a swarm of jaundiced children with bloated stomachs and brittle hair. Sewage trickled down the gullies beside the dirt track that wound through town. I held onto my son, who wanted to pass out the candy we had bought in Antananarivo. How do you divide twenty-five pieces of candy among hundreds of hungry children?

When my husband returned from his lemur search to the hotel, he was surprised to find me crying. It had broken my heart to see children in such a hopeless situation while my robust son, wrapped protectively in my arms, reached out to them, wanting to share his candy stash.

That night, we boarded a train for the ten-hour ride to Tamatave where we were going to catch a flight the next day. Rumors spread through the train that just the day before, Malagasy had rioted against Hindu residents, killing many and exiling hundreds and Tamatave was under martial law. To add to our discomfort, torrential sheets of rain pounded on the steamy windows. There was no food, water, electricity or ventilation. The windows were rusted shut. Only lightning bolts illuminated the train interior at night.

Desperate for a breath of fresh air, I disembarked at one stop by myself and stood in the pouring rain, refusing to get back on. The stress of Third World travel was getting to me. My husband grabbed my arm and yanked me onto the train as it began to move away from the platform.

In Tamatave, we stayed in another whorehouse. It seemed all the "decent" hotels were bordellos. We were beginning to wonder where the other tourists were. By the end of the two-week trip, we had encountered only a handful: two French expats from the nearby island of Reunion and three Russian scientists on leave from their expedition boat. After the French colonists left Madagascar in 1960, the country became Marxist, and closed its doors to Westerners. The doors were beginning to creak open again and it seemed we were among the first tourists allowed in.

As we left Tamatave, it was hard to ignore all the shop windows broken from the rioting the day before. We were flying from civilized madness to Île Sainte-Marie, a coconut-strewn haven cloaked in romantic history, the retirement spot for legendary pirates.

We boarded the small plane, thinking it was our escape to a real vacation. We headed into a tormented sky. The wind god played ping-pong with our aircraft. I crossed myself. I'm not Catholic, but it beat biting off my nails. Touch down we did, finally, right before I threw up. Nobody got off the plane but us, yet people were pushing to get on. We soon learned that a cyclone was coming.

Cyclones are disturbingly loud—like a very angry, roaring and snarling lion. And wet. And they last several days. We were stuck on the island for four days staring at the downpour with our ears plugged. Not a shred of blue sky. At night, we slept under the bed on the concrete floor, afraid the roof would blow off and carry our small son into the heavens. On a positive note, we were served an unlimited amount of lobster for lunch and dinner.

After the cyclone calmed down, we finally got to explore Île Sainte-Marie only to find that the entire island had been flooded and most places were inaccessible. The beautiful white sand beaches were completely covered in debris and fallen coconut palms.

Exhaustedly, we packed up our books, bikinis, and beach toys and off we flew to our next destination but things did not improve. One of our worst days involved a twelve-hour ride sitting on leaky gasoline cans in one hundred-degree heat, bouncing over a pot-holed dirt road. My husband suffered the most, his skin carpeted with an iodine rash from eating too much lobster.

The driver dropped us off in Ambanja in northern Madagascar, a port town with not a single motorized vehicle in sight. The streets were a swirl of livestock, saronged women, wary-eyed men, and throngs of children. It was too hot to be inside at night. Charcoal braziers smoked in front of huts. Our lodging was a bordello dive, but they had beer.

Beer was our savior. We sat on rickety chairs in the middle of the road, swigging Three Horses, the local brew, and watching Galen cavort with a baby goat. I felt happy, ecstatic even. Perhaps this remote pageant of humanity milling before us swathed in bright colors and dark skin glowing from the firelight, was worth the horrendous ride.

The beer not only went to my head, it went to my bladder. I walked giddily to the outhouse and entered the pitch dark. I heard a scurrying noise and turned on my flashlight. Two fat rats eyed my descending bare bottom. I felt too sick to even scream.

The mosquitoes in Ambanja are chloroquine resistant and we couldn't give Galen the other antimalarial drug because it is too strong for children (and probably adults). If one of the several hundred constantly-hovering bugs bit Galen, he had a high probability of getting malaria. We were on mosquito (and rat) alert all night. Buzz, swat. Buzz, swat. Buzz, swat.

The next morning, we waited with others at an inlet for a boat to Hellville, on the island of Nosy Be, Madagascar's only touristy beach resort. The town's name made me uneasy. Why was it named after the Devil's abode? It was the only English town name we had encountered. I wondered what the Malagasy names meant. Tamatave: town of broken glass. Ambanja: land of ass-biting rats?

A whitewashed steamer pulled up after the requisite half-day delay. The ocean was as smooth as glass. Dolphins broke the placid emerald surface. A Chinese family offered us sticky buns and tea. In Chinese-accented French, they told me how the sister boat of the one we were on had sunk a month before. They all turned and pointed. There she was, sticking her nose up out of the water. "Everybody died," they said and continued, "Too many passengers for old boat. Like today... too many."

They seemed calm. Why should I worry? They

weren't. I counted heads and clenched my jaw with every tilt of the boat.

Finally, Nosy Be appeared on the horizon and we were still afloat. We docked in Hellville and checked into a Holiday Inn with clean towels, French cuisine, and movies at night. Ironically, the town with the most foreboding name turned out to be normal. I was bored. After all we'd seen and done, it just seemed so dull.

Some days, during our challenging meander through Madagascar, I was on cruise control just so I wouldn't go out of my mind. At those times, I'd write murder mysteries in my head, pray for a cold beer, clean my fingernails. We came to appreciate the simple pleasures only after we'd had our vacation illusions pounded out of us.

On our last night, a scraggly troupe of Chinese acrobats were in town and, for thirty cents, we watched them balance on top of twenty chairs and do pretzel-shaped contortions.

Would I go back? Yes, but I'd leave my son at home and expect the unexpected. Galen, if he could remember, would probably tell you a whole different story, one filled with odd wonders—bug wings the size of his hand, kid goats frolicking with him on the street, and plane rides reminiscent of Mr. Toad's Wild Ride at Disneyland. I'd have a hard time keeping him from coming along.

RABBIT CHASE

MY ANIMAL TOTEM has always been snakes. I encounter them frequently on hikes and in my garden. My connection to them started long ago. While still a teenager, playing hooky, I fell asleep in a dry creek bed. Suddenly aware that I was not alone, I awoke. A large, weighty rattlesnake was draped languidly over my ankles. Perfectly warm, honey-coated rays of mid-day sun beamed down on the both of us taking a break from the obligations and inconveniences (such as school) of life. I freaked and kicked the snake high in the air—watching it cartwheel through space and then land in a poison oak bush.

That is when snakes started showing up regularly in my life, but, I digress.

While snakes represent transformation, a metamorphic shedding of skin, rabbits represent running away from one's fear. Lately, rabbits were appearing in my life whether I liked their symbolism or not. They even popped up one day on the river.

I was leading a whitewater kayak clinic on the Klamath River near the California-Oregon border. We used two-person inflatable kayaks, with the student sitting in the front while I instructed from the rear. Michelle, who had never been boating before, joined me for her first lesson. She told me she was also a dancer. I decided to teach her a special way I paddle that feels natural and in tune with the river's flow. I call it " Indian paddling," a light, noiseless stroke where the paddle blade cuts into the water seamlessly and the kayak glides forward.

Our paddling rhythm was completely in synch. I felt a team spirit. Our speed increased as we sliced through the water, moving far ahead of the other boats in our group.

We moved forward gracefully—no splashing or echoing of drops. We spoke in hushed tones. The river was moss green. Osprey eyed us as they swooped past on fishing expeditions, argumentative steelhead trout thrashing in their talons.

Michelle said, "It feels like we have done this before in a past life as Native American women." I had that same feeling of familiarity with the river, and of kayaking California waterways in the era before the white man's intrusion.

After a series of tall-peaked, frothy rapids came a long stretch of languid, flat water. I strode the kayak and paddled standing up like a gondolier. We sung the theme song to *Bali Hai* at the top of our lungs. Loudly and out of tune. No one to hear us but the fish and the Osprey. Or so we thought.

Suddenly, the kayak came to a standstill even though we were paddling. In fact, we were going backwards. A Kurok Indian youth was dragging us to shore. He appeared out of nowhere. I knew he was from the Kurok tribe because the Klamath River flows through their reservation and he had the distinctive broad yet chiseled facial features of other Kuroks I had seen in the area.

When he had pulled us into waist-deep water, he plunged under the boat and raised us in the air on his shoulders. We screamed in disbelief and paddled the air, to no avail. He was trying to flip us over. He surfaced and determinedly attempted the maneuver again. Michelle shouted at him jokingly, "Okay, we'll stop singing!" He didn't respond or laugh, just violently rocked the kayak. We threw our weight (collectively, over 250 pounds) back and forth and managed to stay in the boat. He stoically shouldered the kayak, again, and hoisted us skyward. This time, Michelle and I were precariously angled over the water and almost fell out. But we were damn good at high siding, a rafting term for leaning your body weight toward the high side of the boat, and miraculously stayed in the boat.

He dropped us and mumbled, "I can't do I; I can't do it."

Between hysterical giggles and guffaws, it finally dawned on me that this was weird. I looked in his eyes; there was no sign of drug use. I sniffed; there was no alcohol odor on his breath. Then, he went under the boat *again* to tip us over. This was getting old. When he popped up, dripping and exhausted, he furtively glanced up the bank. I followed his gaze. On the cliff above us, standing in the shadow of tall pines, a handful of Kurok elders observed us silently with their arms crossed over their chests.

Behind me, I heard hissing.

I whirled around and raised my voice, "Stop now!"

He closed the kayak's air valve and looked at me, attempting his first grin. This guy was on a quest and we were his quarry. He pulled us into even shallower water and I yelled, my voice raspy from laughter, "Let us go." He did, and then waded to the bank without even turning to look at us. I called out, "What is your name?" He didn't answer. Then I heard him say to the somber men above, "I am too weak—too weak."

Our friends in the other boats had caught up and watched in disbelief, not knowing what to make of this kidnap comedy. They hung back because of our shrieks of laughter. Several thought I knew him.

We continued on down the river and forgot about it. That night around the campfire, I recounted how

I taught my Indian paddling technique that day and then immediately out of nowhere, a real live Indian appeared and tried to seize our kayak. Everyone agreed it was bizarre.

Two days later, we were in Happy Camp at a gas station, miles away from where we rafted, when I heard my name being chanted by our group. I walked toward them. The group parted. They were surrounding a dented pickup truck that was filling up at one of the pumps. Inside the truck, looking a tad nervous, was the same Kurok youth who had tried to tip over the kayak.

I stuck my head in the window, peered into his dark eyes, "Why? Was it a dare?"

"Yep," he replied.

"What is your name?"

"Rabbit," he replied.

"Get out of the truck."

He seemed reluctant, but he opened the door. I draped my arm over his shoulder. Michelle stepped forward and got on his other side. He was startled by this twist toward friendship. We had photos taken of the three of us. He was rather handsome. Everyone started cheering. He then kissed and hugged each of us, and let out a roaring war whoop as he drove off.

Later, when I recounted the kayak story to a girlfriend from New York, she asked why I didn't rip his throat open with my sharp fiberglass paddle blade. She would have. But it never even occurred to me. I was never afraid.

So why the rabbits?

One week before my encounter with this man named "Rabbit," and after much chasing, I rescued a bunny hopping down my street in the suburbs of Marin County and delivered him back to his owner. A week after the kayak incident, I was hiking on a narrow deer trail reflecting on the peculiar event, when my eyes caught sight of a niche in a bay tree. In the hollow was a shrine with a photo of Jerry Garcia, a pair of earrings, torn theater tickets and a large ceramic rabbit. Where were my brave and sinuous snakes!

That night I had a dream, and in it, I kissed my ex-husband. It felt good—which scared me. Completely shaken, I awoke in a haze of dread and misgivings about leaving him. I had just signed the divorce papers. I felt disheartened about life's opportunities that had been abandoned due to my separation. I worried that my decision would hurt my son, would stunt him emotionally. Guilt is a frequent visitor and flavors the moments when I am alone with my thoughts.

My ex-husband is in my dreams a lot. I often feel like crying and wonder if I will ever be in a relationship again. Love is hard to catch, just like a rabbit.

I ran the Klamath River again a few years later. Just as we were putting the boats in the water, a Kurok man appeared and told us not to run the river that weekend. He said there were tribal initiation ceremonies going on along the riverbank and that the river was sacred. We might even encounter hostility and he would not want the shaman's wrath bequeathed on us as we paddled past. Out of the twenty-seven people on the trip, only one man, voted to continue. The rest of us decided to respect the Kurok's wishes.

SURVIVING
THE SALT

I WAS A TIMID, sickly child who stayed home more than went to school and had not an ounce of athlete in me. Oddly enough, decades later, I seem to be blossoming into Amazon Woman, especially in my inflatable kayak.

The longer the trip, the bigger the rapids—the more I say yes! Yes to those wave trains that send me airborne. Yes to dancing around rocks as the white water rushes me toward their hard faces. Even yes to the crisp snowmelt waters as they pour over me while I paddle into a big, hungry, boat-eating hole.

A group of friends and I lucked out and won two permits in a lottery slot to run the Salt River in Arizona. We were going to kayak it in late March and have a support oar boat bring our gear and food on this five-day, fifty-four-mile expedition through cactus canyon wilderness lands.

Several friends had run the river the previous year and waxed ecstatic about the beauty of the desert scenery and remoteness of the river, which is run-able from February through May.

It is an undammed river, so its running season is dependent on the winter snowpack. Fairly continuous Class III and IV+ rapids make it a challenging river. (Class V is gonzo, and VI is certain death as far as ratings go.)

We arrived at the put-in at Mule Hoof Campground after sunset, just as Comet Hale-Bopp arced over the canyon's rim. As we set up camp beside the river, the moon eclipsed, leaving us stumbling in the dark.

That's when I noticed the roar of white water. Suddenly, I felt nervous. How big was this river I was planning to kayak on for the next five days? There was no way of telling till dawn when the sun would shed light on the Salt and I could see my watery highway for the first time.

The next morning, as I was pumping up my two-person kayak, a friendly dog leaped onto the boat and licked my face. He belonged to the Apache police, who were standing behind me in a tight knot eyeing our group.

We were on White Mountain Apache tribal land, and I thought they wanted to collect the permit fee. Instead, they had a request, "When kayaking along the river, could you keep an eye out for this dead guy?" An Indian youth had disappeared the day before after plunging over a waterfall.

The tallest officer said, "If you see him floating, tie him off to something on the river bank and flag him."

"Flag him?" I asked.

"Mark the body with a bright colored cloth so the helicopter can spot him," he explained. "When you get to the take-out down river, notify 911 about where you left him."

The idea of spotting a bloated dead person on our journey did nothing to calm my nerves.

In the frosty morning air, I stood on the bank studying the river. It was wide and fast, and did a slamming turn around the bend, suggesting weight, speed and big rapids. "I've done bigger," went across my brain screen, followed by, "Ha, you're scared. You haven't kayaked this season yet," followed by a realistic, "Breathe."

My kayak buddy, Serge, and I suited up and pushed off into the roiling red water. We are a team and have kayaked several California and Oregon rivers together. Kayaking with Serge is like dancing; he is agile and powerful, brave and playful. We kick ass on the river.

I felt stiff at first. The bend led us into a huge wave train—harmless enough, yet exciting. The waves crested seven feet above us as we paddled to their peak, spilled over the frothy tongue and charged to the bottom, only to be shot up again. The icy water woke me up, and adrenaline—a great drug—kicked in.

Crashing and weaving through a humongous rapid, we would be up to our chests in bubbling white water. When the kayak filled with water, it seemed more like a submarine or a champagne bath. I joked with Serge that we should be wearing snorkels and masks.

I had to adjust my eyesight to differentiate the contours of rock and water; the river was the same red-mud color as the boulders studding it. I was also stunned, and distracted, by the remarkable canyon lands punctuated by marching three-armed saguaros, lipstick pink cactus blooms, and dramatic geological strata of jutting rock walls.

We passed under a ribbon waterfall and noticed the distinct taste of salt on our tongues. Back paddling, we hovered under it, mouths open, delighted with the saline flavor. We had discovered the reason the river is called the Salt. Up until 1940, Indians gathered salt here, and the site continues to have spiritual meaning for the Apaches.

I was still spooked at the thought of finding that bloated body, so whenever the rapids calmed down and the water surface flattened (which was rarely), I turned my attention skyward. This was how I spotted the ancient cliff dwellings and petroglyphs that populated the area near the salt waterfalls. I also observed bald eagles, which the Apaches call "planks in the sky," circling slowly in the air thermals high above us in the vibrant aqua sky.

By the third day, I was getting cocky and my Mighty Mouse attitude arose. That approach got dashed when we flipped in a snarling hole of seething white water that I should have avoided. The next moment, I was somersaulting through what river runners fondly refer to the bottom of holes as the "rinse cycle" in the "white room of doom." One, two, three, four, five... Phew. I got spit out only to find myself under the kayak. At the surface, I gasped for air. The frigid water sucked the energy out of me so quickly I barely had the strength to pull myself and Serge into the kayak.

Before we could catch our breath, the churning waters angrily carved their way through another boulder-strewn sheer wall canyon.

I didn't realize Serge was on the edge of hypothermia from the recent flip until he insisted we run the next Class IV+ rapid we encountered. Not a good idea considering how fatigued we already were. Reason had left him and he was irritable. I knew we should portage and carry the kayak around this section where the river careened around some huge boulders and then did a five-foot drop.

I held my ground, fed him a Power Bar and got him in some warm clothes. Later, he thanked me profusely.

Testosterone isn't needed to be extreme.

A year later I ran the Salt again, but this time it was snowing and so bone-chilling that when I flipped my kayak twice in one day, I suffered from extreme hypothermia.

My fellow kayakers did a rope rescue from a rock ledge I'd been clinging to for an hour. They stripped off my clothes, surrounded me with body warmth and poured some very potent white lightening down my throat.

That night I could not sleep. Dancing and drinking around the campfire, I was ecstatic to be alive. My exhausted companions wanted to stuff me in a sack as I kept them awake all night with joyous, wolf-like howls.

KAYAKS, CASTLES AND KIELBASAS

ABOUT ONE HOUR into the kayak rally I noticed a distinct cultural and apparel difference between the Poles and the Americans. When it began to rain heavily, we gringos wrestled into waterproof neon Gortex as a bathtub raft filled with Poles wearing only faded swim trunks paddled past us. They waved merrily, throwing back vodka shots as golf ball-size raindrops pinged off the water. Around our necks hung expensive sunglasses dangling from Croakies; around theirs, they had shot glasses tied with string.

Four other journalists and I, all of us well-known in the American river rafting community, had been invited to Poland to attend the 54th Annual International Kayak Rally on the Dunajec River that borders Slovakia. This tradition is a friendly competition among canoers and kayakers from all over Eastern Europe. About seven hundred professionals and tourists of all ages and abilities descend the river in a frenzy of activity, to the delight of residents and visitors. It is basically a three-day party over fifty-seven miles of river. Our host and guide for this fete was Yurek Majcherczyk, a world-famous expedition kayak leader. I had read in *Outside Magazine* about his daring-do first descent down the Colca River Canyon in Peru. At 14,339 feet deep, this gorge has been recognized as the deepest canyon on earth by both the *Guinness Book of World Records* and *National Geographic*. Who could say no to traveling with him? My nickname for Yurek became, Never-A-Dull-Moment-Man.

Our group had flown in from New York to Warsaw on Lot Polish Airlines. The French champagne flowed freely in first class. In true California style, I suggested we trade neck massages. Pretty soon, we were all getting neck rubs, including the pilot, who left the cockpit to see what the heck was going on in the cabin. We had him laid out on the carpet and all of us gave him a back massage. The trip was certainly starting off on the right foot.

We were then whisked by train to Krakow in southern Poland, then by bus to the town where the race would start the next morning. At the opening ceremonies and banquet that evening, we were regaled with speeches and toasts.

We toasted each other's countries, the rally, the mayor, the color of the drapes (Communist bordello red velvet), and on and on it went. At one point in the toasting, one of the American journalists fell backwards in his chair off the dais. As he rose, unscathed, to give yet another toast about rivers, brotherhood and sisterhood, little of which was coherent, the Poles grinned good-naturedly at the tipsy Amerikanis, and raised their glasses yet again.

Jib Ellison, fellow journalist and founder of Project Raft, whispered to us that we needed to nominate a designated drinker—*not* the guy who had fallen off the stage already! Jib had spent two years in Russia and said it was the only way we would survive because the Eastern Blocers could drink us under the table. He volunteered for the position and also showed us a neat trick—surreptitiously filling the shot glass with water when no one was looking. We drank a lot of water further into the night unbeknownst to the Poles, who thought we were matching them shot for shot. Jib had a major hangover the next day.

That morning, we organized our gear. Yurek provided us with kayaks, paddles and lifejackets. I had never been in a hard-shell kayak before and felt some trepidation. The river turned out to be a very easy Class II with few rapids. As Robert, one of my paddling compatriots, pointed out, "The only reason you'd capsize would be from gawking too much at the Dracula-like landscape," which included looming shadowy castles and Carpathian mountain gorges. However, it was instantly evident that the point of the race was to have fun. Participants were launching in wooden canoes, racing kayaks, and even kiddie rubber rafts. Once we put our competitive egos (after all, it had been promoted as an international *race*) aside, we had a blast.

The river carried us gently along. Occasionally, we had to pay attention to a minor rapid or portage our kayaks around low-head dams (usually one-two feet high). We passed farms and towns with quaint hand-hewn stone buildings where many roofs were capped with a tire-size stork's nest.

Toward the end of the first day, the terrain of pastoral fields dotted with haystacks changed and craggy mountains reached up from the riverbank to rocky heights. We pulled out between two castles on granite outcrops.

A traveling soup kitchen had been set up for the boaters on the shore. This delightful contraption had four containers filled with various steaming savory soups—the lentil and caramelized onion was rib-sticking good, as was *bigo*, a chunky dish of cabbage and meat. We washed this down with frothy beer and took in the surreal vista of the castles looming above the dark opal-hued waters of the Dunajec.

Satiated and lazy, we were ready to peel off our sticky Gortex layers and wash away the river silt.

After taking a bone-warming sauna at the local inn, we re-joined our fellow paddlers at the kayak rally's huge campsite, and Yurek searched out a group of old college chums he hadn't seen for twenty years. Yurek and his friends had conquered rivers all over Eastern Europe in their university days. They reminisced about cutting classes to drive to Yugoslavia in a rattletrap VW bug and run rivers no one had descended before.

We sat around the campfire for hours, telling stories and singing as a drizzly, damp fog enveloped us. Yurek's friends insisted we sing a song for them in English. Our team of five Americans, not one with a lyric in us, dug about for a tune to sing together to the persistent Poles, who had already regaled us with half a dozen musical tidbits. They not only sang but also accompanied each song with the guitar. Oh, a sad day for us red-white-and-blue, out-of-key gringos!

The best we could do, and thank god the Poles were toasted and roasted on vodka, was "Joy to the World," sung by Three Dog Night in the mid-1970s. Probably the worst song ever to hit the airwaves, but for some reason, we at least had some cohesive ability to sing it. Must have been strong vodka. Did the Poles love it? Yep! We did harmonies, rounds; we taught them the (wrong) lyrics. We survived the night around the campfire with celebratory comradic slaps on the back. One of them even did the Zbojnicki dance— the Cossack-style dance in which they bounce up and down like kangaroos, kicking their legs out from a squatting position with their arms crossed over their chest (knee surgeons love this dance!)— while, accompanied by an accordion, we sang:

Jeremiah was a bullfrog;
he was good friend of mine
I never understood a single word he said but I
helped him drink his wine

What a weird song!

The next day, before the kayak rally commenced, we toured the ominously somber granite castle of Nidzica. Our guide, over eighty years old and hefting a huge clanking key ring, delivered the castle's history in a chanting oratory. The torture chamber with its hooks and racks got our attention, as did the haunted room. Our guide had been working there for sixty years and, yes, he had seen the ghost. He said he almost broke his leg scampering out of the castle when a vision of an armor-clad knight reaching for him with grasping shadowy hands appeared before him on the stone stairwell.

We then reunited with our rally mates at the riverbank to continue the race. We were heading for the dramatic Dunajec Gorge—five miles of winding emerald river between jutting cliffs more than ninety feet high.

Just before entering the gorge, a brief but torrential thunderstorm chased us to shore where a farmer had set up a *kielbasa* (Polish sausage) stand in his cow pasture. We crowded together under the tent canopy, helped the ruddy-cheeked proprietor turn the sizzling sausages on the grill and washed them down with beer. Singing all the while, of course.

We then kayaked through the gorge that acts as a natural boundary between Poland and Slovakia. The lush, tree-lined banks were alive with symphonic songbirds. Occasionally, we would see a border patrol guard with a rifle slung over his shoulder. Yurek warned us not to get out to take photographs or go pee on the Slovakian side because they might arrest us for illegal entry or worse, shoot us when our pants were around our ankles.

That night at the campground, Highlanders (men from the Tatra Mountains) performed the Zbojnicki dance again. One of the dancers was a veritable pogo stick. When the taped disco music came blasting from their boom box, he pulled me to my feet, as he hopped up and down; it was very hard to keep up with him! Especially during the Bee Gees' "Staying Alive." He even looked a little bit like John Travolta in lederhosen. The dance troupe also did an impressive ax swinging, thigh slapping, pushups dance called Thojnkki, punctuated with loud yells and frenzied violin music. Afterwards, we ate succulent barbecued lamb and sang songs (we got a lot of mileage out of the bullfrog song on this trip) around a sky-licking bonfire.

By the last day of the rally, we recognized people we had kayaked, danced, sung and conversed with. We literally bumped into one charming Polish family on the river; our kayaks gently colliding when we hit a small rapid. We linked up, holding onto the edges of each other's boats, speaking a mélange of languages from French to German.

That night, the Polish Canoe Federation presented the awards and we stood on the platform and gave thanks and speeches with an American flag waving behind us on the stage. This is the closest I've ever come to feeling like an astronaut after a successful journey into outer space, or an Olympic gold medal winner. We were the first Americans ever to participate in the 54th Annual International Kayak Rally and they treated us like royalty, even letting us use the prize kayaks during the rally until they were given to the winners. We found this a tad embarrassing as we didn't know we had been crashing about in the trophy kayaks for the last three days until we saw them lined up on stage and Jib pointed and exclaimed in surprise, "That's my purple kayak!"

One guy with a Rumpelstiltskin beard who had participated a total of thirty-four times, said he remembered when the crystal vase trophy used to be filled with champagne and everyone passed it around the room and drank from it. It is a heavy goblet that holds eight bottles of champagne. Many folks kept leaning over to tell me it was "worth $8,000!" The first place winner gets to keep it on his or her mantle at home until the next year's rally. Oddly enough, the Poles never announced what place we Americans took. I think they wanted to keep the goblet in their home territory.

The next day, bereft of the prize kayaks, Yurek took us sightseeing by bus and swept us off to the alpine town of Zakopanne. The landscape was reminiscent of a pastoral oil painting of broad ultra-green valleys hemmed in by snow-capped peaks. The winding country roads were car-less but around many curves we encountered horse-drawn carts driven by costumed peasants. Poland's Old World culture is still intact.

I spied a shepherd's hut in a meadow and we stopped to pay a visit. The shepherd sat on his porch in the sun, drinking raw sheep's milk from a stiff leather cup. He invited us to join him on the rough-hewn bench. Immense Tatra Mountain sheep dogs sat at his feet as he described how they chase off the mountain wolves. Then, he lifted the rustic cup high and offered us a wordy toast in Polish that, translated by Yurek, included, "... my honored first foreign visitors. Crazy Americans who fly far to drink with me." After splashing the pungent, sour warm milk to our lips and passing around the cup, we all agreed that vodka wasn't so bad after all.

THE
MONSTER
DILDO OF
MEXICO

THE THING WAS huge. When Paul pulled it out of the closet and waved it under my nose, I jumped back, jaw open, disbelieving. Dildos just aren't that big!

This mammoth, rubbery love stick had ended up hidden under piles of recycled paper and unclaimed sunglasses in an adventure outfitter's office in northern California, but it originated in Mexico. When I heard this true story, I just had to pass it on, a story that as yet has no end: This dildo keeps showing up at the most unexpected moments—almost as though it has a life of its own.

Paul leads adventure tours to Baja annually. Last winter, the group was heading back to the States and had stopped at a hot springs overnight somewhere near San Felipe. Wencil, one of the trip leaders, is a handyman-sort-of-guy. After fielding a bunch of complaints that the toilet in the men's camp bathroom didn't work very well, he went to investigate.

Something was blocking the flow of water. When Wencil lifted the tank lid, he adjusted his eyes in the dim light and couldn't quite fathom what the object was that was stuffed into the tank. Pink, long, wide. A gargantuan dildo, just hanging out in the toilet bowl tank.

Wencil gingerly removed the obstruction. He didn't want the others in his group to see him sporting this rubber wonder, so he wrapped it in a towel and made sure its head wasn't sticking out. Not knowing what to do with it, he hid it under his sleeping bag and zipped the tent shut.

Sitting around the campfire that night, Wencil was having a hard time keeping this new-found thing a secret. He invited Paul to his tent when most of the others had gone to bed and presented this new addition to Paul. After five minutes of disbelief and a running stream of "Oh my God, Oh my God, Oh my God," Paul, who is very social and loves to stir things up, took the torch, so to speak, and presented it to the people still gathered around the campfire.

After rolling around in the dirt for a while in hysterics, the group voted to place the almighty lingam on the breakfast table and deck it out altar-style for the breakfast crew. Flowers, candles, and beads all adorned the now out-in-the-open phallic totem.

The next morning, the camp chef and her acolytes arose and discovered the altar. For some reason, they didn't think it was funny at all. Was it because they were all women? Or was it because they hadn't consumed coffee yet? A minor war of words ensued, in which Paul took the brunt of the blame, and faced-up to accusations of being an insensitive lout.

Paul decided to have a hanging, a purging. Lynch the plastic terror before anyone else felt traumatized by its gross size and innuendo of sadomasochistic sex. They wrapped a rope around its head and it swung from a tree for the rest of their stay in Aqua Caliente.

When it was time to pack up and head north, the group couldn't just leave the thing there for other campers to ponder, so Paul cut it down and threw it in the woodbin on the side of the trailer.

Everyone forgot about it until the roadblock. The Mexican police were pulling people over and inspecting vehicles. Things went fine as the officers walked around the van and the trailer that held Paul's tour group.

Until one of the officers reached into the woodbin and pulled out the dick.

He stood in glaring sunlight, holding the sixteen-inch-long wand of love in his hand and asked, "*Que es esto*?" or "What is this?" The other officers turned and looked. They laughed uproariously for ten minutes, threw it back in the woodbin, and waved Paul and his tour forward. They didn't really want an answer.

The next morning, as the chef got out half-and-half for coffee, guess what was on ice? Mr. Pink himself. Someone in the group with a sense of humor had decided it was an organ transplant and needed to be preserved, especially since it had saved them at the roadblock, which often requires a bit of bribing to pass through.

It resided in the ice chest next to the eggs and milk until the group reached the border. Because it had been so popular with the last gang of Mexican police, Paul decided to show the dildo to the customs officials. Unfortunately, his Spanish was at the halting, present tense stage. He whipped the dildo out of the ice chest and said, "This is a lethal weapon. Ha ha."

"Weapon?" the officials asked suspiciously. A few hours of explaining (still in broken Spanish) later, Paul and friends were back on the road. This time, the dildo was thrown in the trailer. People were getting tired of it. The novelty was wearing off. The group, who had been touring for two weeks, wanted to get home and get out of the van.

Weeks went by for Paul, with business as usual, including more trips for him and his adventure company. The new secretary back in northern California didn't like the way the office was decorated, so she decided to rearrange things a little. Clean the place up, get rid of the piles of magazines and catalogs cluttering the floor. First, she needed a place to put it all out of sight. The closet.

She saw the dildo.

No one knew how it got in the closet.

She screamed and tossed it—heaved it—over the fence into the neighbor's yard. But it didn't make it over the fence. It got stuck in a tree limb above the office entrance; a definite eye-catcher. It had to come down, but no matter how hard she shook the tree, it was lodged there. Finally, she called Wencil. Wencil brought a construction ladder. The dildo went back in the closet.

It disappeared a month ago when Paul wanted to show me the star of this story. I had come to his office to pick up gear for a river trip. He was miffed; where did it go? Then, last week I asked about it again. Paul dug around in the closet. He gave a grunt of surprise—there it was, back on the shelf beside the office supplies. He whipped it out.

I jumped back, mouth hanging open, intimidated by the size of the monster dildo from Mexico that just won't go away.

DUSTING
THE DANCE
FLOOR

"I CAN'T GO running off to Ibiza to dance!"
My proclamation comes out as a half-hearted whine. Sana has been dangling this invitation in front of me for weeks. She always rolls her eyes in disbelief at my very real and practical excuses for why I should stay home (work for example, family for example) instead of traipsing off to the dance film shoots, festivals, parties, and forays on dance expeditions she organizes. In her mind, ecstatic dance is the only reason to live and takes

precedence over the more mundane details most people wrap their lives around.

Spontaneously dancing has been a condition I was born with. Dancing alone was okay; I'd gotten used to not noticing the critical gaze of the gawkers, most of whom wanted to be dancing too but just didn't realize it—yet. At least this is what I would think to shield myself from their mocking eyes.

In my mid-thirties, by some miracle, I found a tribe like me. People who knew that life *is* too short *not* to dance. Sana was the leader of this posse of colorfully dressed dancing dervishes who smiled as they swirled by in their own ecstatic movement exploration. Being surrounded by dancers who shimmied and hooted when the energy started to climb like a hawk on a thermal—that felt good. Synergetic. Supportive. Crazy good. It felt like I had come home.

Visions of dancers prancing through my head are burst by Sana's gravelly voice luring me to Ibiza to join the pack. She says, "I'll pay your way and all you have to do is dance every night in the clubs to stir up the floor."

The phone line is crackling with static. She must be in a phone booth on a street corner late at night in Barcelona or Havana or Amsterdam. Voices in a muffled foreign language punctuated by car honks, screechy wheels tractioning against cobblestones, all pepper the background noise.

"To do *what*?" I ask.

Sana's voice booms through the plastic receiver, "The German and British tourists don't dance. They just stand around like boring statues of Stalin and get drunk. Ugly drunk. The nightclubs in Ibiza are *over the top*. We are talking Olympic-size swimming pools in the middle of the dance floor and the *best* DJs in the world. The owners want floorshows and the DJs, brought in from all over Europe, want people to dance and express themselves, not be thugs and roily-eyed dopers. They will pay us to fly to the island and stir things up. Wear costumes, get wild, dance till dawn. What is there to say no to?"

She has a good point...

Ever since I've known Sana, she has led a nomadic life following the global party scene. She'd be brought in to create ambience at the big nightclubs in Cancun, Rio, New Orleans, Berlin. She had a habit of linking in with places where dancing until dawn was a way of life. The woman was a migratory dance animal.

I met Sana Parker in Bolinas, a renegade whaling port on the northern California coast. She'd organized a summer solstice bonfire on the beach. Both of us naked, dancing with seaweed roped around our midriffs, seagull feathers woven in our wet hair, still damp from the dip into the freezing Pacific.

Her matted, calico-colored hair curled off her head like Medusa's snakes. Raggedy Anne aboriginal hair flying as she danced, water sprays arcing over the fire in slow motion droplets. She gyrated and swung her hair around like Rangda, the witch in a Balinese trance dance. Stars overhead, drumming, fire-lit shadows highlighting rounded breasts and drum-taut bellies, muscled men's broad ropey shoulders, fire opal hues glinting in the dancers' irises. It was extremely pagan. Sana's parties were legendary.

At first, she did not like me. I was too girly and the guys—she really liked the guys—were attracted to me, not her. She was almost like one of them, a female caveman type. Hairy armpits, loud voice, aggressive, opinionated, strong body odor, violent when she drank. No roses or prom corsages for that girl!

Sana and I were in an unconscious alpha female jostle that night in Bolinas, but we came to an understanding around the leaping and licking bonfire flames. We were both gypsy girls at heart.

The bond deepened and she camped out at my house in California every summer. She'd string a hammock under the fig tree and rarely come indoors. Unless she smelled coffee. She *loved* stimulants.

My ten-year-old son would call and tell me he was bringing friends home and request, "Could you tell Sana not to be outside naked when we get there?" She was naked a lot. Always doing some art project, naked. She painted our basketball court with psychedelic mandalas and dug a bonfire ring in the middle of it. She dove in the pool and then emerged, naked of course, shaking her mane out like a wolfhound. Entertaining for sure, but a tad embarrassing for a pre-adolescent boy to have to explain who the aboriginal person was with paint streaks all over her copper-toned body.

One time she asked a mutual friend and me, "What is your most sexy fantasy?" We responded with fairly normal scenarios. Her answer was a circle of men, laying on the ground, with her dancing in the center wet (and naked), flipping and slapping her tangled hair on their body. Tara and I looked at each other surreptitiously, *really*? No sex, no contact, except hair tips whipping nipples? No competition there! She could have that experience all to herself.

There is a reason she was paid to be the party maestro. She knew how to throw a party and proved it on her fortieth birthday, held at my house on a hot, cicada-throbbing August evening. One of the many spectacles that made it memorable was the large room she built outside on the front patio with two-by-fours and clear plastic sheeting. Fifty celebrants gathered around the structure. She was naked (surprise!) in the center with paint cans surrounding her. When the music started on cue, she lyrically swathed bold primary colors on the plastic walls with a house painter's brush and then danced against them, creating shapes and patterns with her face, fingers, breasts, and thighs.

This was followed by a tequila-fueled-bonfire-daredevil-wish-making ceremony on the basketball court that required all of us to take a swig, yell out our intention, and then do a running leap over the bonfire. Even my son. Move over, Tony Robbins!

There is a reason that even now, more than a decade later, when people are introduced to me, often their response is, "Wow! I went to a phenomenally wild party at your house." Wild was always the keyword surrounding Sana's behavior.

They then ask, "Do you remember me?"

I look at them, shaking my head, and apologetically respond, "Sorry! It was all a whirlwind blur of swirling bodies and sweat. And sometimes cops showing up to complain that people far across the valley could hear the drumming and hollering."

Sana's husky voice interrupts my reverie. The vision of Sana, glowing copper in a wave of movement, flickering around the many bonfires in our short but intense past, fades. She is impatiently awaiting my answer across an ocean of phone lines.

Getting far away from the man I am breaking up with, a possessive and jealous man, seems like a very good idea. Far, far away on an infamous island in the Mediterranean.

I relent, and my answer comes out as a big welcome exhale, *Yes! Buy me a ticket. I can leave immediately.*

We aren't the first wave of partygoers to find their way to Ibiza. In 654 BC, Phoenician settlers founded a port in the Balearic Islands 79 kilometers off the coast of the city of Valencia on the Iberian Peninsula in Spain. They named the harbor *Ibossim* (from the Phoenician *iboshim*, dedicated to the god of music and dance).

Since the arrival of the first muses, this island has been a destination for hipsters of legend from Joni Mitchell and Cat Stevens in the 1960s to Mick Jagger, Paris Hilton, and Seal nowadays. It has morphed into a hotbed for DJs who use the mega club scene in Ibiza as an outlet for presenting new songs within the house, trance and techno genres of electronic dance music. There also exists a genre of dance music named after Ibiza, dubbed Balearic Beat.

I don't know what to expect when I land on this

mountainous island surrounded by a sapphire sea. But I pack my dance shoes.

Sana brings over six dancers from California to dance on the floors of Pacha, Amnesia, Es Paradis, Privilege, and Space.

The clubs don't really start cooking until one or two a.m., but the warm olive scented evenings seduce us into the streets of the old port of Ibiza Town, its ancient bone-white limestone buildings glowing in the moonlight.

During the day the town is deceivingly quiet. But at night the narrow streets are jammed with jetsetters and wannabes from all over Europe.

Sana has clutches of free club passes to handout on the streets. Of course, we don't just hand them out to the voraciously hungry club goers—we dance them out. In a giant rubber band. She came equipped with props! Hula hoops and gigantic gymnastic bands that could encompass a dozen maniac dancers. Sana is relentlessly unselfconscious and committed to our job of promoting the clubs that have paid our way to this pale alabaster island, epicenter of the global party scene. I have to work at it. The fun and endorphins always get me over the hump of *God, this must look ridiculous!* A bunch of adults in skimpy clothing, prancing through the streets in a giant rubber band expanding and contracting as we grab unsuspecting tourists, pulling them into the band with us like an out-of-control amoeba. At midnight, we dine on *mejillones al vapor* (steamed mussels in a pepper vinaigrette sauce) paella, and peasant bread dipped in garlicky aioli that we wash down with copious libations, including full-bodied Tempranillos and silky crisp Verdejos.

Then, as the moon glitters and winks at us across the harbor, we change into white-fringed dance costumes (more Sana props) and it is time to get to work. At Pacha, the *über* large bouncers (why do they all look like FBI agents?) lift the velvet rope, ushering us past the jostling throngs. We study the club layout and decide where the juice is needed. Stirred, not shaken is the idea, though shake we do. The DJs are really into the thump thump techno beat and it initially takes some creative internal convincing for me to feel that invasive, heart-stopping beat that overrides the normal body rhythm and increases the pulse. The club is the size of a sports arena and its sound system generates enough decibels that I'm sure the Moroccans are rockin' out across the water over in Tangier.

Our white costumes turn eerie blue under the pervasive black lights. We appear as floating sea anemones, transparent tentacles dancing Shiva-like through the awed crowds.

One night at Amnesia, Sana dives in the pool (naked) and swims back and forth with the beefy bouncers chasing her (they can't run very fast), yelling for her to put her bottoms on. Topless—okay. Bottomless—get arrested. Go figure.

People notice us in the clubs. Not just because of Sana's prowess as a swimmer, but because we are the only ones not standing around looking bored with a mega drink in our paw. When our dance troupe isn't "dusting" the dance floor, as Sana likes to call it, we are invited to private parties at remote estates high up in the lonely hills on long windy gravel roads. Just as we start yawning and fidgeting in the cramped car, and wondering where the heck we are, lights suddenly appear and a home that has probably been featured in *Condé Nast Traveler* or *Architectural Digest* suddenly floats on a knoll in front of us. I can really relate to Cinderella arriving at the castle in a pumpkin, wearing ripped clothing.

Dancing always transports me to a magical place. The setting of this particular mansion in a park-like setting transforms me from a hard-working single mom, to a queen ready to alight from her dance throne.

A sweep of sparkling stars overhead lights our dance floor—an authentic bullring. Rich people need entertaining. Dancers, bullfighters, we're all the same.

This particular fairytale setting, with Moroccan Berber tents and Cleopatra divans set up around the dance ring, inspires Oscar, a member of our imported dance posse, and me to *really* dance. With passion and strength and vulnerability. No holds barred. The dozens of guests' handsome, chiseled faces highlighted by the torches are all turned toward us in stillness. Watching. Waiting. We blow them out of the water with our sinewy and sensuous acrobatic footwork and aerial dramas. Oscar lifts me and I slowly spin and flip over his back, my arms reaching aloft like raven wings, like Jesus on the cross, like peony petals lush in their exquisite flowering. The pantheon of stars inviting me to reach upward toward the *Little Prince* velvet night sky. Around my hips clings a crystal beaded silk scarf I bought from a belly dancer in Egypt. It refracts the starlight and tinkles softly as we dance up clouds of dust and dried blood. Our dirt dance floor *is* a real bullring. It has been for centuries.

We dance until the apricot sunrise laces through the dawning palette of a pastel sky. Oscar, Sana, Vision Dancer (yes, that is her real name), and I leave and go to a café. The thinly sliced *Jamón Serrano* (salty, dry ham) on chewy bread washed down with a café negro is divine after a night of continuous, sensuous, trance-like movement. The soft morning sun caresses our tired, upturned faces.

I don't see much of Ibiza during the day this trip. Except for the day Sana almost drowns. She pursues the crazy idea to swim three kilometers out to the legendary rock island of Es Vedra. By herself. There is a lot of mythology surrounding this rock in the sea. Some say it is the island of the sirens in the Homer epics or that it's the holy island of Tanit, a Phoenician goddess of fertility. UFOs are frequently reported landing here. Many claim it is the tip of sunken Atlantis.

⠙

Sana Parker did die a few years later when she was still in her forties. She was a pioneer of ecstatic dance, an enabler of free-form dancing. I can still feel her spirit dusting the dance floors at clubs and festivals around the globe. I'm pretty sure she is still not wearing any clothes.

THE CHILEAN CLIFF CARVER

W E MET IN a bullring under the velvet cloak of night. An evening lit by a pale pearl, bruised full moon. This was where I first encountered the pitch-black-haired Chilean who sported a smirk on his perfectly chiseled face. He stared at me while I was lifted to the heavens yet again. Not a human sacrifice but a contact dance performance I was hired to do at a private party on the island of Ibiza in Spain.

The Chilean and I skirted each other on the dance floor. Like matador and bull. I find attractive men dangerous and try to avoid eye contact with them. They terrify me.

Just as I did allow myself to look into his relentlessly piercing eyes, he swiveled and turned his attentions onto another woman. A real beauty. Slowly, they danced close together. Barely perceptible tendrils of steam were rising from their entwined bodies. He then danced with a man. He danced with the woman again. He danced again with the man. Then he danced with both of them at once. They were svelte and sensual, and wielded sly, flirty smiles. In my direction! Provocative. Especially in the flickering torchlight.

He came close again and grazed my bare arm. Red alerts were going off in my left brain. He looked like a heart landmine. Step toward him and my heart would surely be torn to bits.

This inner torment spiced up my dance routine with Oscar, my California dance partner, who seemed to be getting a little jealous that the Chilean was moving into his territory. Party guests were now standing in a circle around him and me, hemming us in as we increased the acrobatic lifts and spins. This hyper performance, fueled by alpha male competition and magnetic physical attraction, went on until the moon, exhausted, fell into the sea that caressed this limestone island in the Mediterranean. Wiping away the fine grit from the bullring that powdered my arms and face, I did not see the Chilean depart. He had vanished on the arm of another woman. Perhaps another man, too. For the best—I was not there to have a fling. I was there to perform.

My dance troupe did do more than dance on Ibiza. Several days after my encounter with the Chilean, in glaring sunlight, we went in search of the sunken civilization of Atlantis. Local lore had it located off the tip of Es Vedra, an island floating offshore Cala d'Hort's bay.

The scorching heat of the sun beating on the steep trail that led down to the bay released intoxicating herbaceous oils of wild rosemary, lavender and thyme that clung to the cliff side. When we reached the sea's edge, salt bream filled our nostrils. It was enlivening to be awake and outside during

the daylight after so many all-night dance extrava-
ganzas in Ibiza's uber-clubs and mega mansions.

As we leaned against the smooth, sun-bleached
limestone boulders in this quarry on the sea's lap-
ping edge, Sana handed each of us a ritualistic tab
of ecstasy. Sana was our group leader and instigator
of all things outrageous. As the zing zip of the drug
effervesced in my bloodstream and my defenses
dissolved, stifled emotions welled up. The secret
burden of my life surfaced.

I had *so* wanted a little girl child. My son was
adorable, but I wanted more kids. The abortion I'd
had several years before due to my ex-husband's
wishes was a sore, a gash still bleeding into my veins
daily. As the heat emanating from the rocks pen-
etrated my tense body, the iceberg-shard tips of that
anguish melted and rivulets of sorrow slid down my
cheeks pooling, in the hollow of my collarbone.

My maudlin grieving was interrupted by a shuffling sound. My teary eyes snapped open and there
stood a young girl with long dark hair. Not a hallu-
cination. Her jade green eyes stared directly into my
sea blue eyes. By god, my wish was being granted.
Who had waved the wand? Drugs are amazing. I'd

always wanted another child, a girl to take to Paris. And here she was!

This little girl even spoke French. Her name was Marie-Claire. We bonded immediately. She grabbed my hand and pulled me up. She wasn't put off at all by the tears streaming down my face or my herky-jerky French. She wanted to play and to show me the crab.

Still holding hands, we walked past my bemused friends who could not figure out how I had suddenly conjured up a child, and waded into a tepid tide pool. She dove down, pale shiny child butt sticking up in the air. She popped up breathlessly and said I *must* do the same thing to see "him." Sure enough, once I did as she commanded, the crab was waggling his antennae eyes at me from under the rock through the murky water. Our upside down antics had stirred up the sand.

She then took me up a trail and around a ledge and we both peed on the dirt. Both of us were fascinated by the yellow streams gushing out from between our legs. Suddenly, hearty laughter startled us. On the boulders above us stood a man who was pointing and laughing. "Papa," she yelled, wagging her finger at him.

The Chilean! The dark handsome dancer from the bullring full-moon party.

For some reason, I wasn't self-conscious about having him see me peeing with his daughter, both of us totally naked. She explained to me that they had a camp beyond the rocks where he was standing.

Marie-Claire grabbed my hand again and ran down to the sea where the gurgling ocean waves sucked in and out over rocks covered in yellow-green algae. She beckoned me to sit on the green seaweed carpet and slide down into the water. A wave caught us and pushed us upward. We slid back and forth with the tide, laughing until tears ran down our sun burnt cheeks.

I'd completely forgotten my sorrows and desires. This happy child had invited me into her world, an enchanted playground of quirky sea creatures and hidden caves.

Then she slipped into the malachite green waters and disappeared. Her silhouette moved below the water's surface. She looked like a mermaid. Then, there was another larger shadow with her. I worried that it was a predator and dove in swimming to her depth. The shadow was her father. They didn't seem to need to come up for air. They showed me how to swim deep with the colder currents. These people were fantastical and mythical, dancing through their watery world like manatees or dolphins or selkies.

Marie-Claire was hungry after all her romping in the water and on land. We followed a narrow path that wound between the skyscraper-size Mesozoic boulders to where they were camping. He had created an other-worldly living space veiled in cream-colored canvas roofs, with thin slabs of pink slate as tabletops, white smoothed boulders for chairs, and Persian carpets that lay over the taupe sand.

The only way to get to their Bedouin-style encampment was by foot down the steep trail, or by Zodiac. As he prepared lunch, he told me he came here from Belgium every year and brought his boat and his daughter. They held court in this old-world quarry for the entire summer.

We grazed on large green olives, Manchego cheese, tomatoes, and fresh sardines. He had a soft yet radiant smile and told me his name was Patrice. He was from Dalcahue in Chiloé.

My mouth dropped open like an attic trapdoor. I was sitting in a dream setting of opaque rock and turquoise sea, without clothes, completely at home with a man who had terrified me several nights before. He was also blessed with a fairy princess daughter who was affectionate, intelligent and gifted.

Yet, this wasn't the reason my mouth was gaping open. It was because Patrice was from my favorite place in all of South America—perhaps the entire world. An island floating off the southern toe of Chile, only accessible by boat or seaplane, and only for six months a year when the savage winter storms subside. A place where the fishermen's wives knit bulky wool sweaters dyed in natural hues from the blood of walnut husks, moss, berries, seaweed, and mushrooms.

I knew Dalcahue well, as I went there many times in the 1970s to import those handspun sweaters. It took several days on planes, trains, ferries and small fishing boats to get there from Santiago, the capital of Chile. Nobody outside of Chiloé is from Chiloé.

His voice pulled me back to this island in the warmer climes of the Mediterranean. As he sliced ripe tomatoes on a stone slab, he shared that he was a ballet dancer and lived in a church in Brussels that he'd converted into an art and dance studio.

Damn!

Why couldn't he be pompous or stupid? Or from Milwaukee? This was all too delicious and tempting (and I'm not talking about the sardines!).

He flipped through a photo album and showed me pictures of his sculptural work. Full-size men and women engraved in the sand on the beaches of Normandy. Tides in the area shift, as described by Victor Hugo, "*à la vitesse d'un cheval au gallop*"— as swiftly as a galloping horse. The tide comes in at one meter per second. When the long tides were pulled in, Patrice filmed the encroaching foamy salt water eroding the Rodin-quality sculptures he had carved over many days. He chronicled the licking away at their curves, the dissolving of their shapes.

As he ran his fingers over the seashell-gray-toned photographs, describing the feel of the sand as he shaped these voluptuous bodies, his voice soft and faraway, I found him, his lifestyle, his family, all excruciatingly captivating.

A spell had been cast and I completely forgot about my friends back on the rocks.

In the late afternoon sun, after more explorations and a nap in their kasbah, Marie-Claire and I wound around the stones littering the hollow quarry pit they called home. There in the amber afternoon light, Patrice was squatting in front of a carving on the limestone face. It was a man and a woman embracing under water as they swam together. Botticelli delightful, da Vinci beautiful. Classic perfection.

As his golden arms and long-fingered hands chiseled these people into the rock, Patrice told me he was involved with the couple I saw him dancing with at the bullring. The sculpture depicted them. "It is complicated," he said. I don't know why he shared this with me but it made me feel very two-dimensional, simple, and boring. And American.

Suddenly, he looked at me mischievously out of the corner of his twinkling eyes and asked, "Would you like to spend the night? My daughter needs feminine company."

Maybe I wasn't so boring after all....

"What about my friends?" I asked in an embarrassing squeak. My vocal chords weren't cooperating. I was scared and looking for the exit. The intensity of the connection wiped me clean of sensibility and instead of feeling a resounding thunderclap *Yes!*, I practically tripped over him as I ran away. I didn't even say goodbye to Marie-Claire.

As I speed-walked past my astonished friends, who were halfway up the trail, one-way conversations bounced around inside my skull. *You would abandon your young son for a life with a bisexual, polyamorous man in cold, gray Belgium?* My mind spun out dramas as fast as it could to distract me from my attraction to this gorgeous man who had just invited me to spend the night with him. I mean, his daughter.

After I plowed over my friends to get in the car, they asked, "He invited you to spend the night? What are you doing here?"

I muttered something about them worrying about me if I didn't come back with them.

In unison, they all chanted, "Stupid! Isn't that what you wanted?"

On my last night in Ibiza, Sana choreographed yet another party. This one took place in an abandoned military fort. She turned each cold cement room into a vibrant temple celebrating various goddesses from Isis to Aphrodite.

Looking up from the flames licking the sky around the perennial bonfire ring, I saw his eyes across the fire's golden flicker. Panther eyes.

The Chilean and I skirted each other through the evening's mayhem of rituals and exhaustive dance-a-thons. I ended up collapsed in a sweaty pile next to him on one of Sana's makeshift temple floors. He draped a pashmina shawl over me as I pretended to sleep. No kisses. No hugs. No sex. No goodbye.

I arose at dawn and Oscar drove me to the airport for my long journey back to California.

I can still see the jaggy edge trim of his thick pitch-black hair framing his face. I can still feel the tidal pull of ultimate attraction. I'm still in love with that artist. Or at least the concept and packaging.

What if I had spent the night in that stone pink-tented wonderland he created? I muse about this every few years. What if I let the artist from my favorite remote island in the world woo me?

At first, I always repeat the same old litany, "No, no! I had to go home to work and take care of my son." But the blanket of reason that vigilantly guards the door to my heart falls off, and the truth speaks in a timid yet convincing voice, "I don't want to be swept away by the murderous riptides of love. No heart landmines for me (even if they are just in my imagination)…"

LITTLE CHICKEN BONE

THE DANCE STUDENT leaves my studio after a private class and I turn my cell phone back on. It rings instantly. A man's baritone voice queries, "Are you the daughter of Maxine Baker?"

"Why, yes, I am."

I had not been in touch with Maxine for several months. She had begun to call me in the middle of the night, buzzed on something, and would "share" convoluted secrets. Such as, "I think my mother was a prostitute." This particular secret was delivered late at night on the eve of my birthday and I thought, "It's time to take a break and not see her for awhile." I knew it was probably more of a belated drunken confession on her part than anything to do with her own mother.

The man on the other end of the phone line coughs and continues, "She is unconscious and dying at the convalescent home where I'm the chaplain—my name is Aaron. She has lived many, many days longer than the doctor expected. He can't understand what is keeping her alive. Is there a prayer you would like me to say to her from you? A goodbye of sorts? It might make it easier for her to let go."

I realize that maybe she doesn't want to pass until she sees me one last time. I am her love child. Living proof of a broken heart many years ago.

"I'll be there in two hours."

I hop in my car and zoom from my studio in Marin County up to Woodland, a dusty, Central Valley nowhere agricultural backwater town. The convalescent home is surrounded by gnarled, sprawling oak trees. It is one-hundred degrees in the shade. The sidewalk is sizzling hot. Down a dimly lit corridor, past half-open doors leading to rooms that radiate a pulsing, underwater-blue glow quietly pregnant with the hushed murmurings of daytime TV, I find her small, linoleum-tiled room. Alone, on the polyester beige-sheeted bed, lies Maxine Baker. Eighty-six years old, hovering on the borderline of death. She is unconscious. I place my hand on her narrow wrist. Under translucent tissue paper skin, her pulse is beating stronger than mine.

After spending time in silent dialogue with Maxine, my half-sister, Vicki, walks in. This is the first time we have met.

I was adopted at birth and never met my siblings. Vicki is warm and friendly and gives me a hug. We like each other immediately. Stories start to spill out as we hold hands over Maxine's still body. I notice an imperceptible twitching in Maxine's fingertips. Perhaps she is uncomfortable that truths are finally coming to light. Little dust ball secrets she swept into dark corners of her life.

Two more half-sisters, Carole and Cynthia, both drably dressed in faded pink sweatpants, enter and the stories build and mount and shock and relieve. We all have snippets of our history that the others do not know. We stitch them together—ah ha's escaping our inherited thin lips as the panorama of our mother's alcohol-fueled roller coaster ride through life comes into focus. Maxine was a pretty good secret keeper and a true Wild Woman. Or should I say, Wild Wanton Woman. She paid bills with her body—the PG&E man, the lawyer, the grocer. The sisters chuckle knowingly in unison.

They do not know that I have a full-blood brother who was also given away in adoption. This tidbit was accidentally revealed to me one time when I was visiting her and she gave the wrong date for my birth.

"I was not born in 1950!" I exclaimed.

Before she caught herself, she blurted, "Oh that was the other baby."

"What other baby?"

"You have a brother."

The sisters are shocked. Just how many children had their mother given birth to? They tell me how she had danced with Fred Astaire. Maxine never told me this, even though she knew I'm a dance teacher. The sisters remember seeing her twirl around the dance studios with him. She was his northern California dance partner. More chuckles and suggestive winks. I thought he was gay....

So that's where I got the dance bug. I show them a brochure of my dance workshops around the world. The cover photograph is me at Burning Man in the Black Rock Desert in Nevada, dancing with my arm gracefully arcing upward to the sky. They say in unison, "'That is the exact pose Maxine would do right before she would pass out drunk." Vicki continues, "Yeah Little Chicken Bone, that was the signal she was going to keel over, so one of us would try and catch her when that arm would raise elegantly skyward. One time, before I could get her, she went right over the balcony."

During our dialog, Vicki continues to call me "Little Chicken Bone."

I'm mystified and ask, "Why are you calling me that?"

"Because until today, that was my secret name for you. I was there when you were born. I remember being in bed with Maxine when she went into labor with you. I was four years old and woke up one night soaked in blood. She had rented a room in a boarding house in San Francisco and we slept in the same bed. Until the blood was spreading everywhere, including on me, nobody had any idea Mom was pregnant."

Vicki continues, "I ran downstairs and found the landlady, who called for help and then Maxine disappeared in an ambulance. I was told she had a chicken bone stuck in her throat."

After a very dangerous delivery (years later, I interviewed the doctor and he remembers my legs being bent and deformed, and that my head was the shape of a zucchini because of the forceps delivery), I was born at Children's Hospital in San Francisco on December 9th, 1953. Maxine walked out and never even took a look at me. My birth certificate says my name is Baby Girl Baker (capital B, capital G, Baker). She vanished up to a trailer in the Sierra and the sisters didn't see her for five years. They were raised by relatives and neighbors. I was adopted privately by a family who's doctor had met Maxine's lawyer at a roller skating rink during her pregnancy....

Vicki then motions me into the hallway for a secret powwow. She leans over conspiratorially and whispers, "I think we have the same father." I'm studying her closely; a short, tubby, brown-haired, brown-eyed woman.

"Really? Why?"

She answers unblinkingly, "We look exactly alike."

News to blonde, blue-eyed, me as I tower a good five inches above her head.

We then re-join the others over Maxine's body. The eldest of the sisters catches my eye and says, "Do you know her spiritual beliefs?"

Reflecting on my first phone conversation with Maxine fourteen years ago, I say, "Why, yes I do. That was the primary topic we discussed when I contacted her after searching for ten years. We share the same idea that god is everywhere and in everything. Our liberal political beliefs are also the same. Weird! I didn't know those were genetic."

Carole peers at the others and nods to them while asking me, "Would you lead the memorial service?"

I gasp, "I barely knew her. How could I do that? She raised you all. Sort of. Why don't you have Aaron, the chaplain who works here, do it? He seemed really nice."

They look flustered. "Who is this guy, Aaron? The chaplain is a woman."

"I don't think so. It was a man that called me today to let me know Maxine was dying. Not a woman. His voice was really low."

They look quizzically at each other and Vicki thoughtfully adds, "Well, she did have a really broad back."

Leave it to Maxine to have the chaplain who was a man in the middle of a sex change.

We sat around Maxine's deathwatch and told stories, mending and hemming the torn mysteries that had kept us apart for forty-nine years. Not many adoptees get to be at their biological mother's deathbed, or meet siblings who are so open, accepting and forgiving.

Right before she died that night, she rose to the surface of consciousness long enough to utter one last word, "Ed." My biological father's name. A man she hadn't seen in forty-nine years. Maxine once told me that Ed was the love of her life but he wouldn't leave his wife even though Maxine had walked away from her marriage for him. Finally, she had slammed the door in his face when she was seven months pregnant with me. "I never want to see you again," were her last words to him. And she didn't.

But I am still here at her deathbed. Half him and half her. Both wild, both gone, both alive in me.

SINGING
IN THE
IRISH MIST

MY IRISH GREAT-GRANDMOTHER was a warbler. Dorothy Norton played the concertina, smoked a Meerschaum pipe, and was always singing. My mom said the house was like living in a small wooden birdcage with a very vocal canary.

Great-grandma Norton arrived in California right off a boat from Ireland in 1890, at the tender age of seventeen. Her family sent her solo to the land of gold promises. She was to find her brother, who arrived several years earlier to work in the mines, and suss out why he had stopped sending money back to the homeland. Her family owned a bakery in Northern Ireland that ensured they could feed their four sets of twins, but the stipend from California was still helpful.

Dorothy not only found her brother who had started a family of his own, she also acquired a sea captain husband. They built a tiny brown-shingle house in Oakland, and she remained thoroughly Irish until she died at the age of seventy-two. My mother remembers that there was always a lap to sit in, for by the time she was born, three generations were living in that same miniature brown-shingle house near Lake Merritt in Oakland. Her grand-mother was always singing ditties, reciting limer-icks, baking soda bread, and swearing in a brogue so thick no one could understand her profanities.

My mom sang around our house, too. Unfortu-nately, the talent and urge she inherited from Doro-thy Norton did not get passed on to me. For one, I've not a drop of Irish blood in me—I'm adopted.

Years of growing up experiencing my family's musical penchant for song, as well as hearing reports from travelers to the Emerald Isle, made me decide to test my theory that all the Irish can sing on a recent trip to Ireland.

The Wild Writing Women, my writing group and travel companions, waltzed into McDaid's Pub in Dublin on our first night on the isle of green. I turned to some curly-haired, friendly lads at the stools nearby and asked, "Can you sing?"

Without a blink of an eye, or an incredulous shrug, off they went into a full-blown song. In harmony, even. Disgusting. I can't carry a tune or even remember more than one verse. This inability to break out into song has turned into a cultural handicap. Go ahead—ask your American friends to sing a song for you. Embarrassed huffs and excuses will ensue, and then finally, after more insistent goading, they might croak out one verse of some inane song like, "Inagodadavida" or "Mary Had a You-Know-What." Yikes! Pathetic.

Back to the pub...

The lads enthusiastically sang their hearts out and then said, "Now it's youse turn."

A memory arose, freezing my vocal chords: The same request only several years ago in Poland where I was invited to participate in a kayak rally. Our team of five Americans, not one of them with a lyric in them, digging about for a tune to sing together to the insistent, drunk Poles—who had already regaled us with half a dozen musical tidbits—until we finally decided on "Joy to the World"—of Three Dog Night fame, not the Christmas carol.

Somehow, now, in a distant pub in Ireland, I did not see that particular song being the godsend for the Wild Writing Women chorus. How long could we hold these gentlemen at bay with wimpy excuses like, "my throat is sore" or "I have to go to the bathroom"?

"Of course ye can chirp!" was their united response of misguided belief in us.

One of the Wild Writing Women finally saved our collective asses by suggesting a patriotic ditty, "The Star Spangled Banner." We knew at least the first several stanzas. The men at the pub joined in. Of course, they knew all the lyrics.

Several pints later, they pointed out in a jolly manner that our American national anthem was originally a poem set to the tune of a popular British drinking song, written by John Stafford Smith for the Anacreontic Society (ironically, a men's social club in London).

Not only could these Irish gents sing on key, they knew our national history in more depth than we did. Well, we had to do better than that to restore respect.

Looking down, I noticed my red leather shoes. A moment of clarity and insight! Humming the theme song to the *Wizard of Oz*, my gal choir joined in and we soared into inspired homemade lyrics that went something like this:

Somewhere Over the Rainbow

Americans can sing...

This was one tune that the blokes at the bar didn't know the lyrics to...

COSSETED AT CROM

GUESS WHO'D BEEN sleeping in one of the Wild Writing Women's beds? No, not Goldilocks...

Our hosts at Crom Castle in Northern Ireland, Lord and Lady Erne, just happen to be buddies with the Prince of Wales and the Duchess of Cromwell. Charles and Camilla slept in one of the sumptuous four-poster beds just a few months before the Wild Writing Women arrived for our week-long stay. No doubt, the couple enjoyed their getaway in the Buff Room, a particularly elegant guest accommodation with fireplace and all. Odd name, though.

There is a secret door in the wall that separates the main castle from the West Wing where guests stay, which was left open for the Royals so they could just pop on over to the Lord's for drinks or tea. We, on the other hand, did not know about the secret entrance until several days after we had settled in, when Harry (Lord Erne's first name) called and invited us to visit him and Anna, his wife, for drinks. We gussied up and waited where he told us to—in the cramped stairwell on the second floor of the West Wing. Odd, again.

A creaking sound of wood scuffing against stiff carpet drew our attention to the wall—it was moving! Just a crack at first, but then the door swung open and there stood the Lord and Lady of the manor with smiles and handshakes, ushering us into their private castle. It was a world of grand, dark wood staircases, monolithic family portraits, and champagne flutes filled with Prosecco (I was disappointed it wasn't French bubbly).

Crom Estate, in County Fermanagh in Northern Ireland, has been the residence and the historic seat of the Earls of Erne for over 350 years. Our host was the Sixth Earl of Erne.

In the stunningly large living room with views over the lawns to the lake, open-armed oaks and herds of fallow deer created a moving diorama, and framed photos of queens and other familiar faces dotted the interior landscape. (*People Magazine* is my reference point for the celebrity who's who.) On the Steinway piano, polished to an ebony gleam, were several photographs of a divinely elegant young woman—think Jackie O. They were all Lady Erne, fresh from Sweden when she worked at the Ford Modeling Agency 20 years before in Manhattan. She was one of their top models before becoming a Lady in a castle. Need I say, a fairytale come true?

Lady Erne engaged all of us in stories of travel and writing. Her husband published a children's book about a donkey and we exchanged autographed copies of our various books including *Wild Writing Women: Stories of World Travel*. They were intrigued with Carla's motorcycle misadventures in her book, *American Borders*. They read it to each other after retiring that night, and had many questions the next morning, when the secret door opened yet again. Lady Erne said they were "all atwitter" over a scene in the first chapter in which Carla describes frolicking naked through the woods in the rain in Southern France with a newfound lover. "Just riveting!" gushed Harry to me, his eyebrows rising and falling rapidly. He had confused me with Carla and thought I was the one running around in the buff.

So how did we end up in this glorious castle in Northern Ireland? Maureen Wheeler, co-founder of *Lonely Planet Travel Guides* and an honorary member of our posse, was born and raised in Belfast. She knew of Crom, and suggested we hold our bi-annual Wild Writing Women gathering at the castle.

Invited to stay at a castle? Who could say no? The idea seemed just right.

From Dublin, we had driven a few hours and crossed into Northern Ireland, all the while fighting the tendency to veer over to the right side of the road. Screams from the other Wild Writing Women sitting in the backseat were quite helpful in keeping Carla and me focused while driving country lanes, barely the width of a fat cow, toward our fantasy destination.

We knew we were close when the castle ramparts peaked over a rolling emerald hill. The road snaked around the hillock, and we all exhaled at once when the full monty in all its grand proportions, spires and arches, was revealed, back-dropped against a misty lough. *Oh my god!* echoed in unison from the women in the backseat.

For the entire week, the *oh-my-god!* reactions continued as we explored Crom Castle's neo-Tudor turrets and crenellated towers stretching into the sky. You just don't adapt that quickly to living in a castle. It's different than a hotel, we realized. We had the entire West Wing to ourselves. Well, except for the ghost.

"Are any of the guest rooms haunted?" I asked Noel Johnston, the castle manager, when he gave us a tour on our first day of the elegant rooms. They seemed perfect quarters for spirits. He hesitated, and chuckled. "Oh, there've been stories…"

He led us to the Rose Room all the way at the end of the hall. Large-petaled, sherbet colored roses spilled all over the wallpaper, the bedspreads, and the curtains. High ceilings, a fireplace, oodles of porcelain *objet* and a bathtub you could drown in.

After I dibbed the room as mine, Noel piped up, "Some folks do indeed see a lady float through these walls...."

I had my antennae out that first night, eyeing any mischievous movements or shadows crossing the walls. But not a hair rose on my arms and I slept un-interrupted. Perhaps the effect of the weighty down comforter and walls as thick as a fortress kept oth-erworldly intruders at bay. I slept blanketed in the history of solitude, and stillness of the Irish coun-tryside.

Mornings began officially with the filling of the teapot, after which we would slowly meander groggy-eyed into the Victorian Conservatory to write. The immense glassed-in structure towered above us like a crystal cathedral. We'd plug in our laptops—a real juxtaposition in this setting—and write, each of us in silence, for several hours until taking a yoga stretch break.

The biggest downfall of being a writer—other than the pay scale—is sitting on our posterior far too much. We combated the sitting with a series of highly un-Victorian poses: legs spread wide, *derri-ères* to the sky, various gyrations. At one point, all the Wild Writing Women were bent over, reaching for our ankles, when I heard a shuffling sound. It was Noel, edging backward out the door. "Methought you women were writers, not gymnasts," he said. We all laughed when he added, "Do youse do this every morning? Very interestin'! I'll keep an eye out for youse next meetin.'"

One day, I decided I felt slightly feverish and needed to retire to my room with tea and books. It was really just an excuse to soak up the rose factor and the delight of having the castle all to myself for an entire day. The rest of the Wild Writing Women went on an excursion. I wandered the stairways in my bathrobe. I luxuriated in that tub, which was so deep that I needed to prop myself up in order to keep my book from going under. The spaciousness, the time, the solitude, the luxury—I felt like an eccentric Royal myself. Castles do that to you.

"There is no place that conjures up in my mind more Irish romance than the wide and fair domains of Crom." John Ynyr Burges of County Tyrone wrote this in his diary when he was a guest at the castle in 1863.

Ol' John got it right. A romantic castle within a parkland of some 1,900 acres, Crom is surrounded by the glistening waters of Lough Erne, which forms one of the longest inland waterways in Europe. The lake is dotted with a myriad of mysterious islands, many visible from the castle windows. Crichton Tower on Gad Island is a stone folly built in1847, appearing to float not far offshore and beckoning us to visit in the motorboat provided for guests staying at the castle. Grebes call from the water grasses, swans hypnotically weave their graceful dance around the edges of the island and herons break free from their tangled root perches to take flight on huge flapping wings of gunpowder blue. Crom is home to the largest heron rookery in Ireland. Truly a living postcard.

Built in the 1830s for the Third Earl of Erne, after the original castle was destroyed by fire, Crom Castle was designed by the English architect Edward Blore, best known for his work on Buckingham Palace. The suggestively haunting ruins of the original castle lie on the shore of the lake. It survived two bloody Jacobite sieges before it burned down.

Two immense yew trees, one male and one female, guard the entrance to the old castle grounds. They have formed a citadel of intertwining branches. Over eight hundred years old, they are reputed to be the oldest trees in Ireland. Legend says that it was underneath this canopy that Hugh O'Neill, Earl of Tyrone and leader of the Irish struggle against English domination, kissed his lady love goodbye in 1607 before taking a ship from Ireland into exile, never to return.

After a few days of drizzly walks, long writing sessions and teatime by the fireplace, jetlag eased and we got curious about our surroundings. Maps came out. Excursions were planned. But the leprechauns seemed to play tricks on our sense of direction. Winding country roads, mysterious turnoffs, un-posted destinations—we saw many things we never planned to see. Maybe that ghost of Noel's had gotten into the car?

Returning from one of our misadventures, Violet, the housekeeper and mother of our guide Noel, fortified us with hearty Irish dinners. Think potatoes (the anchor of all Irish meals) along with lamb and mint sauce. Every plate included a russet.

At first, there was a collective rolling of eyes when the spuds appeared nightly on our plates... *potatoes, again?* Some of us were watching our carb intake. But a few days into our journey we were so enamored by the ubiquitous spud, we gave in and even started buying farl, a bread made from potatoes. We slathered the thick slices with golden butter and it became a must at every meal.

At dinner we quizzed Violet, who grew up here, as had her father's father's father.

Where to go? What to do? What was Prince Charles like?

While serving drinks by the fire one night before dinner, Noel let it leak that his mom, Violet, was a skilled tealeaf reader. On our last night at the castle, she quietly ushered each of us into the kitchen. So powerful were her translations of the wet, loose leaves of tea that clung to the bottom of the Spode cup that not one of us spoke of it around the hearth that night. We kept her insights and prophecies tight to our chest like cards dealt in a game of poker. No one wanted to show her hand. Reveal her future. Violet gave us each something profound to privately ponder as drizzly, mercury-hued rain streaked the leaded glass windows.

THE
WISHING
STONE

"FORTY SHADES OF Green" it is, this land of ancient stone cairns. The Irish people's thick accents slather around their words as rich as the dairy cream they pour on top of the delectable Irish coffees—as smooth and blankety as the dense foam on the head of a pint of Guinness. It wraps around the stories they love to lavish on the visitors, stories and stories and stories piled up like strawberries on trifle. All blended in with the mysteries and legends of their history. Bodies of bones still jagging out of the rocky beaches at County Donegal which, Violette shares is, "just a wee drive to the West. Ye must go see the coast. During the famine they'd walk for days reaching the shore, where the boats were sailing to America only to die right there on the beach of hunger." Her dense brogue unfurls the story of Ireland's tragic past as she lays down plates piled high with of her special boiled potatoes, roast lamb and aromatic mint sauce on the well-polished trestle table for our dinner at Crom Castle.

One blustery night at dinner, we ask Violet about sacred sites. Ireland is a bastion of superstition and magical lore. She says, "Ye must go to the wishing stone right here on the castle grounds by the lake. Me son, Noel, will show ye. Ye need to sit on the stone without touching the earth around it—every part of yer body. Not a limb on the dirt."

One of us asks, "Violet, have you ever made a wish on the stone?"

"No deary, I have everything I want."

Well, we don't feel that way, ambitious American alpha females that we are. We hustle right over there with Noel in the mid-summer twilight.

As he cautiously holds down the electric wire fence for us to step over, we query Noel, "Have you sat on the wishing stone and made wishes?"

He responds, "Oh yes, indeed, many a time, and the wishes always come true."

We each take a turn, folding ourselves on top of the foot-square dome of lichen-pocked granite. In silence, with eyes closed, hawthorn branches pricking our head like a crown of thorns, we wish mightily.

Less than twenty-four hours after my sitting session, my wish is answered in a way I never expected. An email arrives for me that announces I'm going to receive a tidy sum of money from an unexpected source! It is a doozy of conjuring that solves a major financial problem in my life.

This instant response inspires a daily Wild Writing Women pilgrimage to the wishing stone for the rest of our visit.

When I share my surprise results and our daily visits with Noel, he exclaims, "By gosh, I'll have to build a hut over the stone so youse won't get soaked in the mist."

BREAKING OPEN GUADALUPE

THE MOMENT MY feet touch the tarmac, she is with me. Her outline first—the lacy veil, the open palms, the white-gold halo of flames and aura of red roses, her kind eyes looking directly at my heart. She is inside of me, radiating out. But the Virgin of Guadalupe inside me is covered in a dried mud casing.

I can't shake her. She follows me out of the Albuquerque airport into the rental car and along the Turquoise Trail. Her shape hovers in the fog of my peripheral awareness. In Madras, as we step out onto the gravel road in front of an antique store with a wooden porch and rocking chairs, I tell my best friend and traveling companion, Delisa, about the Guadalupe's startling presence and that the focus of this trip is becoming quite clear—to break my heart open. To loosen the chokehold of fear that has kept me protected for decades from the possible torture of true love that may not be requited. The love that gets your hopes up and then leaves one day for a younger woman. Or just leaves because the man is scared of that kind of profound love.

I have always been the one to walk away, never looking back. Many men lay bleeding in the dust on my trail of relationships. I have acted heartlessly, cowardly. One time, while on an Ayahuasca journey where my intention was to increase my psychic abilities and be a true healer to my dance students, I had to emotionally travel through every relationship where I had abandoned and betrayed a man in this lifetime. And ask them for forgiveness. Ouch.

Yet what do I want in my heart of hearts? To passionately love a man without barriers. To be loved this way; to want to die for my man and him for me.

Yikes! I scare myself every time I tiptoe to the edge of this deep longing. I refuse to let love annihilate me, yet...

Why has the Virgin of Guadalupe, the mother goddess icon of love in the Mexican and Native American Catholic tradition, haloed by a garland of blood-red roses, decided to appear in my consciousness? And right when I land in New Mexico to travel to the magic places I return to often? The hot springs, the remote Benedictine monastery, the rutted, iron-red dirt road through painted canyons, the eroded ruins of ancient cultures long gone, peppered with pottery chards laying in their crumbled architecture like hardened bookmarks?

Delisa and I become aware on the drive through the ghostly mining towns leading the back way to Santa Fe, that the image of Guadalupe is everywhere. Think Coca-Cola, think 7-Eleven, think Walmart. She is ubiquitous.

She persistently taps me on the shoulder, lectures to me of love and that it is my last frontier. And she won't give it a break. On T-shirts, wall murals, my mindscape. Everywhere we turn, there she is.

We spend several nights at Ojo Caliente Mineral Springs Resort, ancient hot springs pouring out of the cliff sides. Sulphur, soda, calcium, arsenic, lithium. A potpourri of healing yet poisonous minerals seeping through our pores, beads of sweat gathering as we lay immersed under star-black sky. Tewa Indian spirits roam down the cliffs from the five-hundred-year-old Posi-Ouinge pueblo ruins above.

Delisa and I are both sensitive to the whispers from beyond, to the wisdom and the chaos of spirits knocking on our door.

She shows up embroidered on Delisa's blouse pattern, stenciled on the napkins in the spa restaurant. I pray that the clay she's incased in crumbles, exposing my heart to love and light. I feel my fear of abandonment and wash it over and over, trying to scrub out the grayed stains of mistrust and broken ties.

In the bright light of day, I hike up a dried waterfall bed, sunlight glinting off mica. My guide, Jason, says, "You must meet the poet. We have a poet working here," when he discovers I'm a writer. Back in the dim light of the resort's lobby, I'm surrounded by three attractive men. Jason, hiking guide and

Calvin Klein jean model, who also runs the spa; Mike, the hotel manager, who is really into spirituality and lends me a book on quantum physics; and the poet. They are all fixated on me. It's weird.

Feeling flustered by all the male attention, I retreat to the breakfast table where Delisa is sitting. A scraping of wooden chair feet on Saltillo tile announces the arrival of a visitor to our breakfast klatch. The poet. His agate-green eyes gleam as if he is going to savor a pastry and has his eyes on the first sugary bite. Instead, he recites a poem about the ruins here. A dramatic delivery with voice ebbing and weaving, dancing on the words. It is a pretty good poem. He recites another. I'm getting sucked in. The face is cragged but boyish. Impish. Sparkly. Broad shoulders. Talented, too... even though the missing tooth is a bit distracting. The invitation to join him in his creative-word-play rowboat hovers on the riverbank of temptation, beckoning me.

Toward the end of the day, he gathers me and Delisa up in his truck and wants to take us "to a remote place, one where there are no people." To me, this is just about everywhere in New Mexico, but he seems to think even this place between nowhere is crowded, polluted with tourism.

We bump along dirt roads over grey-green sage desert plateaus, occasionally passing a dusty, dented trailer with a wooden fence around it, but no livestock or humans. Abruptly, the road drops out from under us. It pours steeply down into a vast canyon. He says he used to come here often to bring supplies to a Native American Shaman who had once been his teacher and guide. The poet learned from him the spirit calls and the chants to the four directions. On the canyon floor, we stop. Purple-black ravens skim the canyon rim and caw and cackle as they wheel above us. I look up and there she is, high on the cliff side. Our Lady of Guadalupe in perfect form. I point it out and he says, "You can see that? Only pilgrims can see it. She is not carved there; it is just a watermark or some other stain. I can't see it that well but the Shaman said it is there." The poet does not know that Guadalupe is tracking me. For a reason. He and my heart have a date.

To me she is crystal clear, as if she is carved in bas-relief. I must get closer and carefully walk amid the thick sagebrush and chamise with its heavy-headed, ochre-yellow blooms inking my skin in pollen, keeping an eye out for rattlesnakes.

When I return to the truck at dusk from my meditation, he takes a picture of me dancing on a rock. I'm dressed in moss green with a rose imprinted bronze locket around my neck that I bought at that antique store in Madras. I will never see this photo. Later, I will put a small picture of Guadalupe, cut out from a magazine, inside the locket.

Back in the truck, he and I sit close, legs warm against each other. Fortunately, Delisa is in the back seat and not paying any attention to what is happening between him and me. He reaches over, takes my hand, turning it slowly, and kisses the palm. His moist breath licks my inner skin. Oh my god. My temperature is rising. Struck by passion, wooed by the poet. He is the snake in my garden.

We stop at a cascade of icy spring water gushing from a pipe on the cliff. Standing in a circle around the splashing water, each of us creates a blessing to the earth and sky and each other. A surreal frisson sets upon us and magical, meaningful words pour forth. He chants, I dance, Delisa blesses. We wander down to the riverbank where swallows skim the coppery surface. Delisa says, "I see native people looking down from the cliff at us. Many of them." She is standing on a berm slightly above me and the poet, and without intending to, her voice deeper than usual, she intones, "We are witness to man and woman joining in sacred union on the ancient banks of time." The poet and I stare into each other's eyes, both knowing a miracle is occurring. Now. We are that man and woman. Delisa is our priestess. Rose colored, tall and gorgeous, she marries us on the banks of the Rio Grande River.

He takes us to dinner at the spa. As he holds the restaurant door open and I walk past, he pulls me tight against his tall frame and snap! Our mouths lock as we meet in our first embrace and kiss. A kiss so passionate a woman faints in the lobby for no reason.

We eat dinner and can't keep from roaming with eyes and hands and lips on each other's terrain. Delisa is smiling indulgently at us. She is a four in the Enneagram and a romantic. She is a part of the story of love found and is being a supportive friend. No wonder: I hooked her up with her husband.

Standing outside, in the fragrant blue smoke of the pinyon bonfire lit for guests on chilly evenings, she says goodnight. He and I twine around each other, hugging to keep warm. Lips relentless in their search for the innerness of each other. He goes back to the lobby and returns with a room key. "Would you like to join me? We can sit by the fire in the suite and talk."

Talk? Ha!

His kisses are so fiery they hurt; I can burn up from them. All I am wearing is my locket. He pushes me against the smooth adobe wall, pressing parts of me hard into the clay, imprinting his heat, his intensity carving invisible poetry into the curves of my flesh. I know my shadow still lingers on that skin-pink adobe wall. The handprint bruises on my forearms lasted a week, each one a faded poem.

His words in the morning follow the speechless night. It is confusing. I cannot talk. My heart is everywhere in my body.

Laying next to me, he pulls me close and cries out, sobbing, "Precious, precious Lisa. I love you," followed by, "Maybe we should just walk away and treat this as a dream." Then the longing returns and he implores, "Come to Telluride with me next weekend to a poetry reading."

I can't answer one way or another. I must think about all this. I gather my clothes, and drive to the monastery with Delisa for our two-day silent retreat, planned for months. I write love poems in the chill dusk setting over the Chamas River, golden cottonwoods electric in their turning. At mass, the Gregorian chants bring forth tears. I thank Guadalupe for the beauty, and the breaking open.

I call him as soon as we leave the canyon and there is cell service. I leave a tantalizing message saying yes to Telluride. He calls back. His voice is flat. Uninterested. My stomach caves in. I call him back and ask why he is so vague after our stunningly mystical connection.

"You've gone from one hundred to zero in a minute; I guess there is nothing there. Maybe Telluride is not a good idea," he says, sarcasm searing my ears. How can he so easily make me wrong and needy? Passion is not a curse, yet I feel him placing a curse on the possibility of us.

Back in Santa Fe, I cry over dense Mayan chile hot chocolate at Kakawa Chocolate House, Guadalupe opening her palms to me on the image on my mug, of course. Swollen tears splash on my dark blue silk blouse. Delisa tries to comfort me and says, "He is just a chickenshit terrified of love."

My heart aches and trembles in disbelief that this man did not want what was between us. The gift of passion and possibility. On the phone he also told me, "Funny that it has been a year of not meeting any women who interested me, and last weekend I met two on the same day: you and another woman, a student writer who is living close by in Abiquiu. You live far away; this is simpler."

My nightmare is born. He has met another woman, younger probably. Maybe.

Why, Guadalupe, did you not deliver me into the sacred arms of love? Why am I abandoned yet again? Can't I tell another story? My upbeat, positive self cheers me on, "Because you are meant to believe in yourself and be truly independent in this lifetime." Crap, crap, crap.

Guadalupe, why? The red clay is drying and the color fading to the dull hue of fallen rose petals as I mud up my heart, again.

EPILOGUE

OVER HALF A century old and only half a globe explored. And then there are the inner soul realms and the deep blue ocean that I love to float and bob in as shadowy creatures glide below. Delicious, mysterious depths still to discover.

Painful clouds of insight into my heart were a surprise side effect of writing some of these stories. It hurt to write, particularly the love stories. The mirror of my words reflected back to me my actions and how some of my travels were driven by fear of rejection, my need to run instead of stay, to wander instead of settle. To be the one waving from the train window as a loved one cries goodbye from the platform.

I look away, my map already unfolded again in my lap. Its veined roads crossing pastel territories beckon me with an enticing finger towards possibility, yet another adventure, or lover, or friend.

If you are concerned that my son decided to become an accountant, safely ensconced high up in an office building in Somewhere America because of all the crazy situations I dragged him through while bumping along in Third World countries, he didn't. He works six months a year for Sequoia National Park and the other portion of the year vagabonding and climbing mountains. Perhaps you'll meet him on the edge of some Patagonian glacier, volunteering at an orphanage in Cambodia, flying a kite on the roofs of Bundi in India, or floating through the Mekong Delta on a leaky bamboo raft.

Enjoy these gems from the wild life I've lived and continue to traverse. Read them out loud to your kids, your partner, and your friends. Write some of your own. Whether you're in Berkeley or Botswana, the story begins when you wake up in the morning and walk into another startlingly brand new day.

ACKNOWLEDGEMENTS

WHAT WOULD I do if I didn't have a great friend in Delisa Sage, who loves to read? She was my editor-in-chief who vetted which of my many stories ended up in this anthology. If you don't like one of them, contact her. Not me. I just followed her email directives:

Duh!

Of course you should put this story in your anthology. It is fabulous! It does need to be tightened up. A few less adjectives. It is so much better as its own story. Xo, Delisa

Everybody needs a literary—or even just a literate—best friend. So I'll also throw into the appreciation mix my Wild Writing Women cohort, travel mate and business partner, Carla King, and my generous-hearted love interest, Jordan Scott, who really knows how to salsa! They both let me bend their ear with a story or two...

And what about the perfect editor? Amberly Finarelli's editing treatment was like icing on the cake. Not too sweet, just the right thickness—but not heavy-handed, yet consistently persistent about where those commas go.

Lyn Bishop is a book cover designer deluxe who came to my house several years ago during a Wild Writing Women meeting about our anthology. We debated what we wanted on the cover and decided it was a map of the world on a woman's back. I volunteered, ripped my shirt off, and she photographed me in the living room. She used this element on the cover for *Wild Writing Women: Stories of World Travel*. To this day, a fabulously classical design.

When it was time to get the feel of the cover for this book, I called Lyn. We worked out the design over Skype because she was in the heart of the jungle in Corcovado National Park in Costa Rica saving leatherback turtles…or was it that young biologist?

And then, the interior. A book needs a midwife. Someone to bring it into the light. Or in other words, get it ready for the printing presses. Who to trust with the design of the interior of my book?

The right font, the perfect dingbat? Yikes! Just the technical skills (and program cost) involved in In-Design are enough to scare a self-published author away from this final frontier that needs to be crossed in order for the story to become a *real* book. Joel Friedlander of Marin Bookworks, kicked this book over the goal post and into reality. Viola! You are holding it in your hands...

ABOUT
THE AUTHOR

THE DAY SHE turned eighteen, Lisa Alpine moved to Paris. She waitressed in Switzerland and picked olives in Greece, paddled the Amazon River, and created Dream Weaver Imports, a South American import company with two retail stores and a wholesale business in San Francisco.

In 1983, she gave birth to Galen Marc Alpine. That same year, she founded and published *The Fax* newspaper in Marin County, California. She then went on to be the *Pacific Sun*'s Getaway columnist for more than a decade. During this period she also freelanced for Frommers' *America on Wheels, Common Ground, San Francisco Examiner, Los Angeles Times, Chicago Tribune, Mothering Magazine, Paddler Magazine, Physicians' Travel & Meeting Guide, Specialty Travel Index*, and many other publications.

With her writing group, the Wild Writing Women, she co-authored *Wild Writing Women:*

Stories of World Travel published by Globe Pequot Press.

She is the Global Getaways columnist in Examiner.com and teaches travel writing at The Writing Salon in San Francisco and Berkeley. For the last two decades, she has also led a plethora of writing and dance workshops in Hawai'i, New Mexico, Italy, Mexico, and France.

Lisa recently started Good to Go Media with Carla King, a venture that helps authors get their books out of their head and into the marketplace. They offer workshops and co-authored the *Self-Publishing Boot Camp Workbook: Ten Steps to Self-Publishing Success*, which they, of course, self-published.

She is currently working on several new titles including, *Wild Blood: Horse Thieves and Whores*, an embellished nonfiction about her renegade birth parents. On a completely different track, *Journey Into Movement: Dancing Lessons From God*, will be a book about the body-wisdom she has gleaned from twenty years of teaching dance as an ecstatic and healing art form. When not wrestling with words, exploring the ecstatic realms of dance, or waiting for a flight, Lisa is planting fruit trees in her garden in Mill Valley, California, or orchids in her jungle hideaway on the Big Island. Her gardens of vivid flowers and abundant fruit remind her that the future is always ripe with possibilities.

To find out about her dance, writing, and self-publishing workshops, go to www.LisaAlpine.com and www.SelfPubBootCamp.com

I would love to know your thoughts about this book after you have read it. Which stories did you like, or even dislike, and why.

Please consider sharing your comments, feedback and questions on the testimonial page on my website.

You are also most welcome to purchase more copies of *Exotic Life* from my website. It is available in hard copy, PDF download, and Ebook formats for epub, Kindle, Sony Reader, and Palm Doc.

Place your orders and log your comments on:

www.lisaalpine.com

Wild Writing Women: Stories of World Travel

This anthology of 24 true travel tales by 12 alpha females is published by Globe Pequot Press and available for $16.95 at www.lisaalpine.com

Lisa Alpine is a member of the Wild Writing Women and the cover model.

WWW authors are daring and intrepid travelers. On the other hand, they can be languid and seductive, or sometimes simply seducing. The nature of the observations and the quality of the writing make this the most distinctive and appealing travel anthology of the year.

—Tim Cahill, author of *Pass the Butterworms: Remote Journeys Oddly Rendered*

Self-Publishing Boot Camp Workbook:
10 Steps to Self-Publishing Success
Lisa Alpine and Carla King

Whether you're a new author or a published author, you have got to be thinking, "There has to be a better way!" Yes there is. This 87-page workbook walks you through the 10 steps you need to complete to get your book project finished and in the marketplace.

The insights, information, tips, worksheets, and checklists in this workbook make this the essential guide to successful navigation through the complexities of your publishing project. The method is simple: When all the tasks are checked off, your book is published.

Order it directly from SelfPubBootCamp.com

Writing: Your Passport to Life

This online magazine is offered to those of you who aspire to write, in the hopes that it aids you in fulfilling that dream.

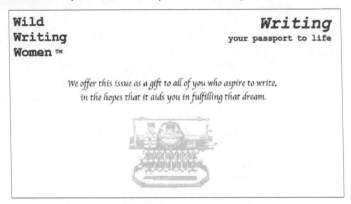

Taking Flight: For First Time Travelers

The Wild Writing Women provide first-time travelers with all you need to know to spread your wings and fly.

Published by Wild Writing Women LLC

Get these and other Wild Writing Women Magazines free on the website at WildWritingWomen.com

Browse this lush full-color magazine free online

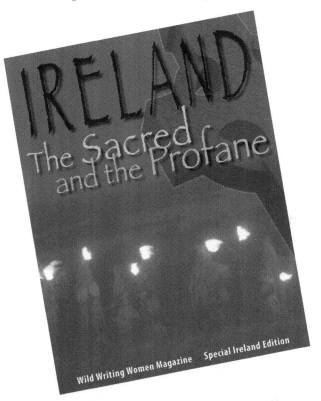

This multimedia exploration of Ireland is a fabulously colorful experience delivered in PDF format with over 250 pages of full color photos, tales of adventure, practical tips, plus audio and video clips for hours of full immersion in Eire.

The stories include off-the-beaten-path accounts of ghosts and midnight fire dancing, wishing stones and the unexpected benefits of Guinness, coupled with practical travel tips, linked resource lists, and reviews, events, and excursions.

From definitions of the word skeltering to the best Celtic tunes for the journey, you'll find that the Wild Writing Women share their expertise in voices irreverent, humorous and unique.

Published by Wild Writing Women LLC | http://wildwritingwomen.com

Made in the USA
Charleston, SC
04 September 2010